TH

ENTREPRENEURSHIP

M000048147

PRAISE FOR THE TAO OF ENTREPRENEURSHIP

"I keep this insightful book on my desk constantly and refer to it any time I want 'just-in-time' inspiration.   Marcia brilliantly articulates how spiritual principles underlie all the day-to-day issues today's entrepreneurs face – and helps us see the truth behind the circumstances. In today's complex business world, this book provides the guide you need through the sometimes rough waters of business ownership. You will learn how to overcome obstacles - once and for all - and reach new heights in your business that you didn't even know were there. A 'must read' for every entrepreneur!"

--DAVID NEAGLE, MILLION DOLLAR INCOME ACCELERATION COACH

"This book inspires us to work with our hearts as well as our heads. It is a gift to all of us who hunger to bring our whole selves to our entrepreneurial work."

--RICHARD J. LEIDER, FOUNDER, THE INVENTURE GROUP
& BESTSELLING AUTHOR OF *REPACKING YOUR BAGS* AND *THE POWER OF PURPOSE*

"There are plenty of guides on how to DO entrepreneurship, but very few on how to BE an entrepreneur. In *The Tao of Entrepreneurship*, Marcia Bench provides simple, thoughtful lessons on developing an entrepreneurial spirit. It's the perfect resource to start your business day with a few moments of inspiration or to help you get through the rough spots on your entrepreneurial path."

--C.J. HAYDEN, AUTHOR, *GET CLIENTS NOW!*

"Every entrepreneur needs encouragement along the journey of growing a business. This book not only offers you unconditional encouragement but also thoughtfully reveals the necessary mindset for entrepreneurial success."

--MICHAEL PORT, AUTHOR OF *BOOK YOURSELF SOLID* & *THE THINK BIG MANIFESTO*

THE TAO
OF
ENTREPRENEURSHIP

52 Lessons in Applying Spiritual Principles to Business Ownership

MARCIA BENCH

The Tao of Entrepreneurship:

52 Lessons in Applying Spiritual Principles to Business Ownership

Published by High Flight Press 2009

Copyright © 2009 by Marcia Bench
All rights reserved.

Reproduction or translation of any part of work beyond that permitted by the 1976
United States Copyright Act without the express written permission of the copyright owner is unlawful. Requests for permission or further information should be
addressed to Permissions Department, High Flight Press, 8269G SW Wilsonville Rd.
#188, Wilsonville, OR 97070.

This publication is designed to provide accurate and authoritative information in
regard to the subject matter covered. It is sold with the understanding that the
publisher is not engaged in rendering professional services. If legal, accounting,
medical, psychological, or any other expert assistance is required, the services of a
competent professional person should be sought. Client names have been changed
to protect identities.

Library of Congress Cataloging-in-Publication Data:
Bench, Marcia
        The Tao of Entrepreneurship: 52 Lessons in Applying Spiritual Principles
to Business Ownership
        / Marcia Bench
        1. Entrepreneurship 2. Business 3. Spirituality
        ISBN 978-0-9817005-3-3

Printed in the United States of America

Dedication and Acknowledgements

I dedicate this book to my students, my staff, and my clients – past, present and future – who are stepping into their role in transforming the planet, just by being who they are and saying "yes" to their guidance.

I acknowledge my husband, Jay, for his endless support of my work.

I must also express my gratitude to my coach and mentor, David Neagle, and the many other people who have contributed to my spiritual growth and understanding as well as my business expertise during my 20-plus-year career.

And I celebrate the God within each of us and the new ways it is unfolding as we move into the planetary and evolutionary shift toward the new global spirituality in business.

May you discover the best self you can be by using these lessons in your daily practice.

--Marcia Bench

TABLE OF CONTENTS

Introduction and How to Use This Book

Dear Reader,

There are lots of how-to books on the market (I've written some of them!) instructing you how to start your business, how to market it, and even how to sell it. But there are precious few books that really help you take on the *mindset* of the entrepreneur. And literally none that help you become *purposeful* in your business – that is, living your life purpose as an entrepreneur.

Starting and growing a business is about much more than just taking the steps of giving it a name, writing your business plan, setting up your web site and creating products (although those are all important components). Truly successful entrepreneurs also bring their purpose to their work, every day.

"Tao" means "the way." The purpose of this book is to help you adopt the thinking patterns, the mindset, and the attitudes shared by the successful, Purposeful Entrepreneur™. You will find that owning a business is truly a way, a path, not just a series of activities.

I have spent more than two decades learning the lessons shared here, and have coached hundreds of clients and spoken to tens of thousands of people about them. But not until now were they compiled into a form you can use as a daily and weekly guide to reinforce this new mindset – and use it on an ongoing basis.

For many of the lessons, I have provided definitions and origins for the words used to enhance your understanding of them (as opposed to our common use of the terms) and to deepen your learning.

This book truly came through me, not from me. I believe it is the Divine speaking to you through me, with important wisdom that will make remarkable changes for the better in your business – whether you are just starting it or are a seasoned business owner.

How to Use the Lessons

I recommend that you read through the book once lightly, perhaps turning to the topics that particularly appeal to you right now and reading them first.

Then, use the book as a year-long template for Purposeful Entrepreneur™ development, taking one lesson each week and reading it in the morning as you begin your day. Reflect on it, and take it into your meditation if you have such a practice. Notice what issues it brings to light in your daily business activities. If you look for it, the word of the week will help, challenge and inspire you.

I wish you success, fulfillment, and the glorious unfoldment of your purpose in your business and in the world.

--Marcia Bench

1

Desire

What do you truly desire, deep within your heart? Are you living that life, fulfilling that dream, doing that work, right now?

Desire literally means "of the father." This is the voice of your highest self beckoning you to a new future.

Desire is the seed of any business. The entrepreneur starts a business based on a desire to fulfill a dream to do business differently (perhaps following corporate disillusionment), to have more fun, to increase his/her fulfillment and sense of contribution, or just to try something different than he/she has done before.

As your desire beckons to you, how will you respond? Will you believe the small thinking of non-entrepreneurs around you that "you can't start a business now," "what makes you think you can do that?," "is there really a market for that?" or "can you really make money at that?" Or is now the time you will finally "go for it" – and claim your own brass ring?

Author Raymond Holliwell has said, "No desire is felt until the supply is ready to appear." That means that the very fact that you have a desire to start a business - or to change or grow one you already own – means that *the means to fulfill your dream already exists, right now.*

Common thinking says to be sure you have the money *first*, before you hire someone or go on that trip or invest in a web site. It would tell you to wait till the timing is just right before you jump.

Hogwash.

NOW is the time for you to move, if you are feeling the desire to do so. Your desire is your Inner Voice, your Divine Inspiration, telling you that your unique gifts are ready to express NOW in a new way – through your own business.

All that is required of you is that you *decide* – "I AM going to start this business, I AM going to invest in that educational program and learn the new skills I need, I AM going to meet with that successful business leader and learn what I can from him." Once you decide, then the money, the people, the resources, the time - whatever you need - will appear, in perfect time.

The first step to success as a Purposeful Entrepreneur™* is to identify your desire, and give voice to it. Tell just one trusted mentor, coach or colleague what you really want… and that you are going to take the steps to bring it into reality soon. (But don't spread the word to the world just yet…) How does that feel?

"Once the desire is clear, the way will appear." Giving voice to the desire will likely inspire you with one next step you need to take in the direction of that desire. You won't get the whole plan at once. When you know what that step is, and have taken it, you are ready to move on to the next lesson.

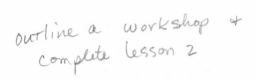

outline a workshop +
complete lesson 2

*The term "Purposeful Entrepreneur" as used throughout this book is further defined in Appendix A."

4

2

Trust and faith

There is a type of entrepreneur who steps out in full trust in his own human abilities, relying exclusively on his intellect and drive to achieve to launch and grow his business.

That is not the kind of entrepreneur I am talking to here.

To be a Purposeful Entrepreneur™ requires that you have faith that Something bigger than you is really "running the show." You may or may not call it God — it may be Mother Earth, Universal Spirit, or just The Presence... but for you to feel confident that this desire you have is your destiny, you must know that it is coming from the highest part of you, your Higher Self.

Once you clear that hurdle, you can relax into the unfolding of your business, knowing that you are being guided, led and inspired by this presence into the highest and best version of what you are here to do.

You will be asked to trust this Presence, both initially and as your business grows.

Think of it as a practice, rather than an event.

Every day, with every task, you have the choice to come from your head or from your heart, to act from Spirit or from your (sometimes limited) human knowledge. And virtually every time you act from Spirit, things will come out better than you could have hoped.

In what do you have faith? Do you trust that Something wiser than yourself is guiding you in your business as well as other areas of your life?

We are not talking about any specific religion here. Rather, we are suggesting that you trust in a Power, an Entity, or a Force bigger than you that is beneath and behind all that happens, and all that is created. Your particular practice in connecting with that deity or power is a personal choice.

When you walk this path of trust, it is as though you are walking along a path on a foggy morning. You can see the next step in front of you, but you won't see the one after that until you take the one you *can* see. But as you do so, you trust that there *will* be another step, and another, and that the destination is your goal, whether it is launching your business, filling your coaching group or practice, enrolling people in your seminar, or achieving a financial goal.

Trusting in a bigger plan than you can see gives you the courage to dream big, to go after *all* of your desires and goals, and to know that you are supported every step of the way. This is important because each time you reach a goal or achieve the fulfillment of a desire, another desire and an even bigger plan will emerge.

Nature's essence is ongoing expansion, ever more life. So you can release the expectation that someday you will "get there" – and trust that you'll always be in the process of "being there."

How much can you trust the unfoldment of your dream?

3
Courage

Entrepreneurship is not for the faint of heart! It takes courage to say what you want – and go for it. "Don't die with your music in you," as the quotation by Peter Duggan goes. But it may feel safer if you never let it out!

Suppressing your dream and "playing it safe" is the equivalent of playing not to lose. You will be much more successful – and experience much more personal power too – if you play to win instead.

Courage is "the ability to face danger without fear." Entrepreneurship is not so much about danger – at least not the way the cavemen experienced it! But since 7 of every 10 new businesses do cease to exist beyond their first 2 years, you must have the courage to overcome the odds, to make it "in spite of," – and to not worry about what people think of what you're doing.

Everything worth doing in life takes courage: asking that special someone out on the first date, standing up in front of the class and giving a report, confronting someone you love about what's bothering you, moving to a new city – or finally admitting "I can't take it any more" as an employee and starting down the path of business ownership.

The word "courage" comes from the Latin root meaning "heart," a common metaphor for inner strength.

To have courage in your business and life is to follow your heart.

Entrepreneurs are an independent group... they have strong opinions and are usually eager to voice them. (Of course, this is also why they get fired from traditional jobs so frequently too!)

Starting your own business finally gives you permission to do things *your* way, to set *your* policies, and to reap the rewards for the risks *you* take. Once you have the courage to give voice to your desire, it doesn't feel like a risk as much as something calling you to take action. The time comes when it is more painful to try to fit the square peg in the round hole – and conform to the corporate mold – than it is to step out on your own and carve your own destiny.

Fear and courage are actually opposites. Fear makes you play small and shrink from the task, whereas courage beckons you to your greatness and urges you to expand. You may find you have to walk through the fear to discover your courage.

When you do, courage gives you strength to stand up for yourself, your own dreams and desires. And the rewards are many. You finally experience the fulfillment, creativity and self-expression you have longed for, but which can only be found (for the true entrepreneur) in your own business.

4

Overcoming fear

Notice that the title of this lesson is not "eliminating" fear but "overcoming" it. To eliminate fear entirely is to stop growing – and all of life is either growing or dying, there is no in between.

To continue to grow, then, whether you are starting your business, stepping it up to a whole new level, or launching a new product or service, fear will arise. You are hard-wired to experience fear whenever you step into something new. It is actually part of the process!

The question is what to do when you feel it.

The dictionary defines fear as "alarm and agitation caused by expectation or realization of danger." Once again, "danger" is not the wooly mammoth charging us, but simply our feeling unfamiliar with the experience we are facing.

When you feel fear, the first thing to do is to *stop*. Breathe slowly, ask yourself what you are afraid of, and watch with a sense of detachment as your inner self provides the clarity you seek.

It is important to stop because fear will literally paralyze your mind – and especially your creativity – if you allow it to dominate your emotions. It is physiologically impossible to make good decisions or to think clearly when you are under the influence of fear. So don't try to!

If you imagine all of your prior experiences as being contained within a bubble called your Comfort Zone, then this new experience – e.g., starting a business after being an employee for a dozen years – would be outside the bubble. It feels like you don't have your bearings, that you don't know what to do – and the thoughts of disaster and ruin can quickly take hold and cause your stomach to tie itself up in knots.

At such times, simply acknowledge fear as though it were an old friend: "Oh, hello fear, I see you have come to visit again." Notice where you feel the fear in your body. Can you isolate the sensations as being in your stomach, on your sweaty palms, or in another place? If so, close your eyes and send light and healing energy to that part of your body. Invite it to speak to you, to tell you what it is afraid of.

Then, ask your Wiser Self this: "What do I need to know, or whom do I need to meet, to bring this experience within the realm of my Comfort Zone?" Wait for the answer. It will surely follow.

Then, take the action you are led to take. If it is helpful, make a list of the worst things that could happen if your fears came true, and then rank them as likely or unlikely to occur. Ninety percent of what we fear never comes about anyway... but confronting it head-on can remove most of its power over you!

Finally, shift your attention from the fear to the dream, your desire, the thing you want to do that has brought the fear into your consciousness. Concentrate on the reasons why you want to do this (e.g., start a business), the benefits it will bring you, and what is exciting to you about it.

Then ask yourself: where did the fear go? Answer: the fear dissolves when you focus on what you love, the positive energy of your idea, the reasons you know it will work – versus the fear that it won't.

Love always dissolves fear. Being on purpose, and taking action to express it in your daily work and life, allow you to be pulled into your purposeful business, instead of derailed by the inevitable fear that will arise from time to time.

Allow the fear to serve you, not to stop you.

5

Creative expression

To start and grow your own business is to say "yes" to your inner creativity – to be willing to allow it to express through the products and services you offer. Raymond Holliwell put it this way: "Business is an expression of man's highest aim, man's religion."

For some entrepreneurs, this means "building a better mousetrap," improving on existing technology, or filling an unmet market need with a new product or service. For others it means inventing something new. But in each case, four things are true.

First, there is nothing truly "new" under the sun. Every invention, every new technology, every innovation, comes from arranging pre-existing elements, ideas and concepts into a new form. This should encourage you! You do not have to "create something out of nothing"; you simply need to rearrange what already exists into a form that appeals both to you and to the customers who will buy it.

What you need already exists; you simply need to listen to your inner guidance to see how it needs to be blended, arranged - or turned upside down! – to become the service or product you have imagined.

Second, the purpose of your business is creative self-expression. One of the primary motivators of the Purposeful Entrepreneur™ is to find an outlet for the ideas and creative energy pent up within him/her. You have likely been frustrated in past work experiences that others would not listen to your ideas for how things could be done better, streamlined or enhanced. You *knew* you had a great idea – but "they" did not find your idea to be within the company's policies or mission or goals... so your ideas were dismissed.

In your own business you finally get to give voice to what is important to *you* – and no one else can tell you "we don't do that here" or "I don't like that idea." It's up to you! And fortunately, what usually happens is that your audience - your client base – so enthusiastically responds to what you share that it is even more rewarding than if you had offered it through someone else's company as an employee. They often wonder where your offering has been all these years!

Third, your creative expression comes *through* you, not *from* you. You know that Something greater than you is guiding the process. And when you write or speak or draw or sing or create or invent or interact with customers, it is the Ultimate Muse, the "Divine Download," that you receive and that is moving through you, expressing itself as that activity.

This means that your job is to say "yes," to be open, and to release all distractions and resistance that would keep you from being a clear channel through which the Divine can flow. (This is also what we do as coaches: show up, be fully present, bring our best coaching skills to each session – and let the magic of the coaching space do the work.)

Finally, creative expression, for you, is not a luxury but a basic need. Others among your family and friends will not understand this – so don't expect them to! You need to express yourself creatively just as much as you need to breathe, to eat, to sleep and to hydrate yourself. Without an avenue for the creative energy within you, you develop a

kind of "creative constipation" – and its side effects include unsatis-
fying relationships, unfulfilling work, physical illness or disease, and
overall emotional malaise. The dammed up energy of unexpressed
creativity simply finds another substitute outlet... or turns on itself
physically, emotionally or relationally.

Key !

As you learn to trust the wisdom within you, know that you have
a high calling on your life, and that expressing the creative urges you
feel is an important part of that. Being a business owner will give
you the freedom, the space, and the avenue through which to do this
most fully. And your clients' and customers' eager response will be
its own reward!

16

Energy

Everything in your life and business is energy – the pure, raw creative force, awaiting your thoughts and emotions to be impressed upon it and create the tapestry of your life experiences. And that includes your business.

The chair on which you are sitting, paper on which you are reading this book, the inspiration that created the words on the page, and your business concept and its implementation - all began first as energy before they became tangible form.

Energy becomes perceptible through thought, and thought coupled with desire (emotion) then becomes the thing that was thought about. In its raw form, energy is neutral – neither positive nor negative. But truly, "thinking makes it so." If two people experience a situation – e.g., the economic downturn of 2008 – one may consider it a tragedy, and the other (the entrepreneur, of course!) an opportunity. Whichever way the person views it becomes true – it is a self-fulfilling prophecy.

Henry Ford was able to visualize the V-8 engine before it was invented. And in fact, when he charged his engineers with inventing it, they told him it was impossible. Every month, every quarter, they would come back to him and say they could not do it. But he said he WOULD have a V-8 engine, and to keep working on it. After about a year, they finally did it. What if they had quit before they got his desired result?

Similarly, if your business is experiencing a slow-down of customers for a product that has traditionally sold very well, you can view it several ways: as something that is wrong and needs to be fixed, or (possibly) as an opportunity to reinvent the product, improve it, move into a new market, or even create a brand new product line that is more aligned with your customers' present and future needs. It all depends on how you look at it.

Though the dictionary defines energy as "capacity for working or acting," the term was first used by Aristotle to mean "force of expression." People with high energy will tend to overflow their enthusiasm and ideas to those with lower energy. And in dysfunctional relationships (in both business and personal realms), people with lower energy will suck the energy from those who have more of it, creating a co-dependency. High energy is very magnetic!

As an entrepreneur, you likely have higher energy than most people – indeed you must in order to persist in bringing your idea into reality! What you must be wary of is attracting people whose role in life is to be energy sponges, rather than contributors to your business. They can make your work much more difficult as your reserves are absorbed by the sponge instead of being shared with those who will take it and use it in their lives.

Take time to be grateful for all the forms in which energy has manifested in your life – and in the infinite possibilities it offers for the future.

How will you harness the energy available to you in the next greater expression of who you are, both in life and business?

18

Being an entrepreneur

Just going through the steps of starting a business may satisfy the dictionary definition of an entrepreneur. But there is much more to it than that.

To truly "be" an entrepreneur means to take on the traits, the mind-set, and the behaviors of an entrepreneur. If you have been working for someone else until now, you will need to make some radical changes in your thinking to be both comfortable and successful as a business owner.

Being an entrepreneur means giving up any tendency to blame others or outside circumstances for what isn't working. It means taking charge of your own destiny, and being proactive in anticipating market shifts, inviting change, and taking a stand where it may be unpopular.

As an entrepreneur, you will also have to release any old beliefs that someone else will take care of you. In the Manufacturing Age, people thought the company would take care of them and fund their retirement.

We no longer have that luxury.

In the Knowledge Age, and especially as a business owner, you must plan for your future, provide yourself with health insurance and other benefits —decide when you will take vacation, and do it!

Another employee mindset that prevalent in corporations today, which you must also abandon, is the so-called "entitlement mental-

19

ity". People start to slow down, to learn less, to contribute less – to rest on their laurels – after they have been doing a job or employed by a company for a few years.

The true entrepreneur, by contrast, is committed to lifelong learning, to staying ahead of the curve, and to promoting innovation within her company as well as within her life.

 You are paid to take risks – not to avoid them.

Your customers, clients, and others will look to you as a leader. Are you ready to assume that role?

If, as Tom Peters has said, the corporation as we know it will not survive more than another decade or so, what will take its place? Think about what you complained about as an employee: the long hours, the lack of focus on people and their families, the closed-mindedness, the lack of new ideas. You can change *all* of that now. But will you?

What would your business look like if you had the perfect balance between personal and work life? A constant stream of innovation? Close attention to your customers and their changing needs? Full expression of your gifts and talents?

Nothing stops you but your limited, outdated thinking.

Be an innovator. Be an entrepreneur.

8

Decision

B eing "wishy-washy" has no place in the Purposeful Entrepreneur's™ life or business.

Every successful entrepreneur is earmarked by the ability to make decisions quickly – and to change them slowly.

It is the making of a decision that unlocks the door to the supply that is ready to appear so that your vision can manifest. If you have been wondering where the money is, wondering where the clients are, or why things aren't moving forward – it is likely because you have not actually made the decision to have them. (I know you will want to argue with me here!) You may want them, wish for them, even need them – but until you *decide* to have them, they will not come.

Decision comes from a Latin root which means "to cut off." When the early explorers arrived at a country, some of the expedition leaders would actually burn the ships that brought them there as a way of cutting off escape. That certainly provided motivation to make the newly discovered land work for them!

Once your decision is made, you must then adopt the mindset of the person you wish to be. For example, if you make the decision to earn $100,000 or more this year, you are then charged with acting like a $100,000 business owner, making decisions and choices like a $100,000 business owner, and living the lifestyle of a $100,000 business owner. Would such a business owner be handling her own email? Setting up product links in the shopping cart? Doing her own grocery shopping? Working in a cubbyhole in the corner of a messy spare bedroom? Or staying at a discount hotel or a friend's house while attending a conference?

The decision and the actions which follow will usher in a whole new level of experiences (and, in the case of the above example, revenue). But decision must come first.

Sometimes it seems nearly impossible to decide between two options which appear to be mutually exclusive. When this happens, apply this question and see what new possibilities may emerge: *Is there any way for me to have both a and b?*

I have applied this "both/and" approach numerous times in my own life with delightful results. When it seemed that I had to stay in a city where I no longer wished to live to obtain medical treatment for a serious illness, while we were simultaneously building a new home in another state, I asked this question. I had assumed there were no suitable medical professionals in the new location – but one day felt guided to check to be sure. It turned out that state-of-the-art treatment was available in the new location, and we were able to live just a few blocks from the construction site and make changes and inspections as needed during construction – and I got my medical treatment too.

My mentor, David Neagle, suggests these four questions whenever you are making a decision about something:

→ Is this something I want to be, do or have?

Is being, doing or having this thing consistent with my life purpose?

Is being, doing or having this thing consistent with the Laws of the Universe?

Does being, doing or having this thing violate the rights of others?

The answer to questions 1 through 3 should be yes, and the answer to 4 no, for you to proceed.

Once you make a decision, your subconscious programming will immediately begin to intervene to keep you in your pre-decision state. It will help to expect this in advance, so you do not take it as a sign that your decision was incorrect! Your opportunity here is to hold steadfastly to your vision and to the decision you have made. Just like when learning anything new, it will take conscious practice for a while to embrace the new mindset (e.g., the thinking habits of the $100,000 business owner instead of the struggling start-up owner), until in time they become second nature.

Making a decision "for" one thing may mean making a decision "against" or "away from" something else. And when that something else is what is comfortable and familiar, it can be difficult!

Decide for your growth, your unfoldment, and your magnificence. You are worth it!

Intuition

Do you consider yourself to be intuitive? Entrepreneurship will require you to trust your "gut" – also known as your intuition. If something doesn't "feel" right, you should not do it.

Intuition is defined as "the capacity of knowing without the use of rational processes." Rational means reasonable. So when you act on your intuition, it may not seem reasonable or logical – in fact, it often doesn't!

What often blocks us from listening to our intuitive hunches is questions like these: "What will people say? How will I justify that action? How can I act when it doesn't make logical sense?"

What other people think is of no concern to you – you are here to fulfill your purpose, not to fulfill their expectations. And you don't have to justify the decisions you make as the Chief Entrepreneurial Officer of your company. Intuition usually *won't* make logical sense – especially since you will initially only know the next action to take, not all the other pieces of the puzzle that will follow.

Your intuition, at its essence, is simply your Higher Self speaking to and through you. You may know what someone is about to say. You may find yourself thinking about someone you haven't talked to for years and feeling like you want to call them — and when you do, you find out they have exactly the knowledge or contact you need for the next project you are going to start.

Intuition also speaks through your body, perhaps as a tightness, a pain, tingling, chills, or a feeling of hesitancy when considering doing something. Receive it as simply your Higher Perspective on the situation, trying to save you money, time, or heartache by stopping you before you start.

Each person's intuitive language is a bit different from everyone else's. Learn your intuitive language by paying attention to all the dimensions of it: colors, feelings, what sensation you "always" get when you are inspired or being cautioned. Sounds, words, images, thoughts... all of these are components of this language that is unique to you.

Every time — without exception — that I have acted against strong intuition, I have been extremely sorry I ignored it. And it has cost me relationships, money, and time.

Intuition is not the opposite of the intellect, but a complement to it. Intellect on its own will stick with what is safe, what is known — and what is logical. If you are committed to grow through the path of entrepreneurship, experiencing breakthroughs as you go, you will need to learn to listen to *both* intuition and intellect.

Intuition can directly access what intellect requires many steps to do.

It is like going through a file cabinet one file at a time until you get the one that starts with "h", versus going right to "h" without having to examine or complete steps "a" through "g". How much more quickly could you and your business move if you didn't have to take the preliminary steps to your goal?

You can increase your ability to listen to your intuition by noticing little things you are already doing through this avenue. When the phone rings, instead of jumping frantically to answer it, take just a moment to go within and see if you can identify who is calling (without looking at the caller ID of course!...). You will cultivate an ability to know this more and more often.

If you feel anxious or uneasy before an appointment, or during the day for no apparent reason, close your eyes, go within, and ask your inner self what you would like to know about this feeling and its origin. Also ask if there is any action you should take in response to it.

When making an important decision – whether business or personal – check in with your first impression or inclination – your intuition about the situation – before you rationalize that impression away. Analysis is fine, but just as customers buy based on emotion and justify their purchase with the facts, you must decide based on your gut instinct – and defend the decision (if required) based on analysis.

And it's also all right to just say "I don't want to go that direction" and stand solidly in what you are feeling guided to do. You don't owe anyone an explanation.

Pay close heed to your intuitive urges – every successful entrepreneur does.

10

Promoting your business

Your deepest inadequacies about who you are, what you deserve and your self-esteem will arise the minute you begin promoting your business and selling your products. Have you noticed?

The trap is that most of us are taught that "you are what you do" – so if someone rejects your creation (your product or service), they are rejecting you. In truth, the two are separate. Someone who says no to your product is saying no to your product, not rejecting you as a person.

Take a breath, and take this in. You are *not* what you do!

You are much more than that.

Think of your business as a laboratory in which you are going to do a series of experiments and notice which ones lead to your desired result and which ones don't. You can take the same attitude Thomas Edison did, after hundreds of unsuccessful trials in working toward inventing the light bulb, when he said that "I have just discovered 990 ways *not* to invent a light bulb."

He did not assume something was wrong with him because experiment 951 did not work. He did not blame it on having low self-esteem or not deserving to be successful.

He simply took the objective attitude of a scientist and went on to trial number 952.

Can you do the same with your product launches, web pages, site selection, proposal writing, and other activities in your business?

Being an entrepreneur means being willing to put your best work out to the world, and attracting those people with whom it resonates and for whom it has value. You need not be concerned with the rest of the world that would prefer another company's products or is not yet at a phase of their development to see value in what you offer.

Mastering marketing and selling principles is a lifetime endeavor. You are not expected to know it all – or even a substantial part of it – when you start your business. Most entrepreneurs are good at making things or providing services or doing whatever the work of the business is – but are unskilled in marketing, business development and selling.

The good news is, marketing and promotion can be learned. (And much of it can also be outsourced or delegated, once you understand what the primary emotional benefits of your offerings are and how best to sell them.)

But you must build the bridge between what you sell and who will consume it – and that bridge is marketing.

The ideal promotional approach will result in pre-qualified customers approaching you, versus you chasing people and trying to "sell" them.

It's a different game, especially in the current Knowledge Age.

Take the action you need to take to become comfortable with participating in the promotion of your own products and services.

Get a coach, attend a seminar (or several), read books on marketing and human psychology. Practice in front of a mirror, or with a video camera or a close, supportive friend. Try something, and don't be too upset if it doesn't work.

Babe Ruth and others after him that broke home run records also broke strike-out records.

View marketing and promotion as a game – and make up the rules as you go! Seek to fail as fast as you can... your success is right behind it.

11

Your customers, your tribe

Whether you know it or not, you are connected energetically with the customers of your business - past, present and future.

It always amazes me when a coaching client brings to the session the very same issue I am grappling with in my own life or business, expecting me to help guide them to the answer. This is when it is abundantly clear that it is the coaching that does the work, not my human knowledge – since I usually haven't entirely worked the issue out for myself yet!

This phenomenon is just another example of how we often "teach what we most need to learn."

Once you leave your family home, each stage of your life, each place you live, each company in which you work, will give you the opportunity to choose a new family or "tribe" to which to belong. You will feel the most in common with people who are experiencing the same kinds of challenges, illnesses, needs or problems that you do.

Often, you are called to be a leader, healer and teacher to those who are just a few steps behind you on the same path – who are facing the issues you have already begun to master. For example, people often approach me about how to write and publish a book, since I have completed more than 20 books. This is also why I have taught career coaching for many years: I first did it, and the next step was to teach it.

And this principle is not limited to services such as coaching. Your products will be most appealing to those who have similar preferences, proclivities and tastes to yours. Have you created a better "mousetrap" out of frustration with the old designs? Then others who share a similar frustration – and desire for a better way – will resonate with your product, and buy it.

So now that you understand this connection you have with your customers or clients, how does it change how you approach your marketing, your promotion, and your new product or service development? First, notice that if your evolutionary journey and theirs are one, then the issues you are experiencing now – which may be natural sequels, if you will, to your initial product or service – are the same ones they will be feeling a need for in a few months or years.

Notice how you find your way to the solution. Pay attention to the emotions you feel, the challenges you face, and the process you go through. Journal or otherwise document it so that you can empathize with your customers – and also glean key pain points for your sales letters and other marketing material.

This will require an ability to observe yourself as though you were a third person – a "witness" if you will – and will help you be more objective about your own difficulties. Remember how Edison did this? Witnessing your process opens the doorway to the attitude of experimentation, the life-as-laboratory attitude that is the precursor to huge breakthroughs. What are you inventing through your life and work today that will serve your tribe in the future?

Also notice that if you and your tribe/target market are one, the ideal relationship will be a two-way dialogue. They will tell you by their response to your offerings whether you are centered, clear and connected to them – or off base. They will also communicate by unsolicited emails and calls, as well as responses to customer satisfaction surveys, how well you are hitting the mark with them – and what they want next.

If your customers are not responding the way you wish them to, the issue is not with them, but with you. Where are you ignoring key messages from your inner self about new directions you need to go, changes you need to make, habits you need to break, etc.? What do you need to let go of that is no longer working?

Your customers or clients become, in this sense, your teachers. They are your intuition in human form. What are they telling you?

12

Self-direction

N ot everyone is suited to being an entrepreneur. Some people simply need more direction from others and more external structure than is provided by owning your own business.

When you start your work tomorrow morning, you will not see a memo on your desk or computer dictating your priorities for the day – unless you wrote it to yourself! Being a Purposeful Entrepreneur™ means knowing your purpose and incorporating it into not only the essence of your business, but each day's priorities, activities, meetings, communications, and scheduling.

If you were fully living your purpose in your business today, how would the quality of your interactions with others by email and telephone change? How would you *think* differently about the staff and customers of your business?

The Purposeful Entrepreneur™ is guided by her Higher Self, in the sense that the business and its activities are divinely inspired, but also by her lower self, her human self with its talents for organization, goal-setting, planning and management. This path is about integrating both your Higher and lower self into your business.

If you focus only on the Divine, it never becomes form. If you focus only on the facts and circumstances of your business, there will be no sense of higher purpose or vibrational resonance among your customers – nor will you feel completely fulfilled. Both are needed for the business to thrive.

Even at the beginning of a business, there is always plenty to do. Being self-directed means setting and re-setting priorities throughout the day. The question is not "How much did I do today?" but "How much did I progress toward expressing and fulfilling my purpose today?"

If you only do the next thing that is in front of you - without considering what would bring you most joy, what would take you most directly toward your purpose, or what would best leverage your strengths – you will burn out quickly.

Practice making plans for the day with a priorities list of no more than 20 tasks – and then be open to it shifting if more important things arise. Be sure the top 3 items on your list are truly the most important. (And don't sabotage yourself by starting at the bottom of the list, just for the sake of demonstrating *some* sense of accomplishment!)

Self-direction, for the entrepreneur, is like the pan in which you bake a cake: it gives it its shape, its form, its appearance. Without it, all the luscious batter would simply be a gooey mess on the counter!

Channel your energy into a form that is pleasing to you – your business, and the plans you make for each day. Adjust when necessary. Course correction is a part of self-direction, and is the earmark of a successful business owner – as well as a successful astronaut, since the spacecraft are typically off course up to 90 percent of the time but do eventually reach their destination.

Before you make your to-do lists for the day, spend a moment in meditation. Close your eyes, breathe deeply, and ask your Higher Self for inspiration and guidance as you plan your activities. Then, make your list from that higher perspective. Better yet, make a "to be" or intentions list for the day instead! You will often find you save time, energy, even money as you let the higher wisdom within you inform your familiar planning structures.

13
Risk

Taking risks is part of being an entrepreneur.

According to the dictionary, risk is "the possibility of suffering harm or loss." Notice that it does not say the "probability" or "certainty" of suffering harm or loss – just a possibility. How large that possibility is – and how likely it is to occur – varies widely.

Most people think of entrepreneurs as taking a high degree of risk – "going for the long shot."

Not true.

Yes, we want big wins. And yes, we have big dreams. But the savvy entrepreneur thinks carefully through the worst case scenario ("what do I have to lose?"), the best case scenario ("what could I possibly gain?"), and the likelihood of each. And then she takes an informed risk – often moderate in nature – and many times succeeds.

It often takes mental rehearsal of the planned action – whether quitting your job and starting your business or approaching that celebrity about endorsing your product – before you are ready to take the physical act. Each time you practice doing it and don't actually act, the pain of not doing so increases.

Eventually, you feel like a tightly stretched rubber band, being pulled in two directions. One is the path of safety, familiarity, and sameness – the other is the path of apparent risk, the unknown, and newness. But this second path also carries with it a great degree of excitement.

Your growing edge is the thing that excites you the most – and scares you the most – at the same time.

Sooner or later, the excitement of the new will outweigh the fear you have felt of the unfamiliar, of actually taking the action – and what once felt like a risk will now feel like what you *must* do. If you don't, you know you will miss out on something big... and to refuse to take the action is to risk living with regrets.

What you or others see as risk is simply your Higher Self calling you to more life. Life is forever expanding or contracting, living or dying – there is no "holding pattern," no in-between place.

Where are you being called to more life today? What new direction is your purpose taking you in your business? Can you be quiet long enough to listen to its guidance – and then act on it?

Risk is a part of life... you cannot escape it. You take a risk driving to work every day, allowing your children to play sports, or saying something difficult to your loved ones. But it is a question of whether you are ready to step into a new set of risks – one that will take you where you really want to go.

14
Contribution

You are here on the planet at this time to make a contribution. It is a contribution no one else can make, as it is unique to you.

We usually think of contribution in the sense of giving to something or someone, and that is one definition. But the kind of contribution you are to make through your business evokes the second dictionary definition: "to act as a determining factor."

This meaning implies that by doing the work you were meant to do, by starting and growing the business you were meant to own, you influence what is going to happen in the world, and in your customers' lives. To say it another way, by stepping into your business, you proactively transform some key aspect of people's lives.

If you contribute to a conversation, you co-create it. Similarly, as you contribute your gifts through your products and services, your customers' lives are changed... and they in turn influence others. Thus that transformational factor plays out.

So if you thought going into business for yourself was selfish, think again!

Your life's purpose *must* express as your life's work — and for you, the Purposeful Entrepreneur™, as the unique products and services that comprise your business. Otherwise, you will be depriving those who could benefit from what you offer of the contribution you could make.

As you release each new product and each new service, as you work with each new customer or client, it will help if you view the transaction as though it were an offering being laid on the altar of life. It is sacred, a heart-felt gift going to your customer with love.

Give your contribution with love – but do not be attached to what the customer does with it, whether they use it the "right" way, or whether they use it at all.

Your responsibility is to offer your gifts; it is then up to them to take full advantage of what they have purchased.

Contributing your gifts is saying "yes" to the life force within you that is longing to express. Refusing to do so is saying "no" to life – and dying in some small (or perhaps large) way.

Check in with yourself now. Do you feel any impulse to try something new, to create something different, or to perhaps repackage or refocus something you released in the past? Are you being guided to contribute to new and different people as your customers or clients?

It is up to you how you respond: with a "yes" or a "no".

15

Persistence

It is not enough to come up with a great idea; for it to become a successful business, it must be put into action. And then, still more action will be needed to bring it fully into form.

The test for the entrepreneur, at every turn, is: can you stick with your dream, even when people laugh or ridicule you, even when it is hard, and even when things don't go as you would like them to?

This takes strength of character — what author Napoleon Hill calls an intense desire, coupled with definiteness of purpose. In *Think and Grow Rich,* Hill says, "Those who have cultivated the HABIT of persistence seem to enjoy insurance against failure." [emphasis in original]

So if you are struggling with fear of failure, concerns that things won't work out — then persistence may be your answer.

To persist is "to continue firmly and steadfastly despite obstacles." Can you do that?

In fact, once you make a decision to do something — especially if it represents a new level of income, a higher vibration in your life, or an expanded concept of your business — the first thing that will happen will be an obstacle! Your subconscious will fight, claw and otherwise work its devious tricks to keep you right where you are.

Can you persist in spite of these obstacles, keeping your sights on your goal?

There is a difference between insanity and persistence. Insanity has been defined as "doing the same thing and expecting different results." That is not what we mean here.

You cannot reach your bigger goals, or solve the problems you now face, if you try to use the same mindset that created them. That will simply yield more of the same results you have been getting.

Instead, you must adopt a whole new paradigm – in short, you must grow. In *You²*, Price Pritchett tells the story of a fly buzzing busily against the window trying to get outside – when the door is open just on the other side of the room. The fly can be persistent in his efforts to fly through the window, but it will yield him nothing but fatigue and, ultimately, death.

Adopting a new paradigm is like the fly turning 180 degrees and flying out the window. All of a sudden the struggle stops and he is free again! What if you could find that same freedom in looking at something radically different than you do, and then holding to *that* vision, persisting until you attain it?

Be careful what you are being persistent about. If you have been doing the same thing for months or years and it hasn't worked, it probably won't work now either.

Try something else.

16

Vision

For the Purposeful Entrepreneur™, vision is a verb, not a noun. Having a clear vision of what you want your business to look like, how it will be staffed, what products you will offer, what income you will be making, and the like is an essential component for success.

Tom Watson, Founder of IBM, is said to have used this principle throughout the growth of the company. He and the management team simply created a detailed vision of their desired outcome when the business was complete. Then, they measured each day's results and activities against that vision.

Your vision is the mold for your new – or growing – company.

This type of vision does not rely on your physical eyes, but on your inner eyes – your imagination. At least one psychological study found that an imagined experience is every bit as impactful as an actually experience. They divided a group of basketball players into three groups: one practiced shooting free throws at the gym every day for 30 days, the second group did mental practice (visioning) of successful free throw shooting, and the third group did nothing during that month. At the end of the month, the improvement of groups 1 and 2 was almost identical.

A "vision" is "a mental image created by the imagination." Just having the idea of your business being created in the first place was a vision. Now, as you prepare to grow it, you can use that same ability to pave the road in advance for new products, new customer groups, a new store or office, higher income, or whatever would be pleasing to you as an improvement to your current business.

The only limit to what you can create is your imagination: how big can you dream?

It often takes coaches, mentors or other visionaries to help us see a bigger vision than what we think is "practical" or "realistic." Go beyond the realistic: what do you *really* want, if money, time or resources were no object?

One thing is for sure: if you cannot envision it, it will never happen. Once the vision is clear, the path to its unfoldment can begin.

By taking a moment to envision a perfect outcome to the difficult conversation you need to have, or seeing a client have a breakthrough in your mind before holding a coaching session, you will be much more likely to experience the actual result you have envisioned. Visioning is a kind of "pre-staging" of the desired result. It gives laser focus to an otherwise diffused energy.

It is also important to think of your vision not as something you have to make happen, or struggle to clarify, but rather to receive. Clearing your "channel" to perceive and receive it will allow it to unfold.

Think of your vision as a muscle that must be exercised, stretched and used in order to stay healthy. Let it surprise you with its images as you allow space for it to guide you to the next steps that are possible for your journey.

17
Harmony

For you to attract anything into your life or business, you must come into harmony with it. Everything in your life now – the people, the income level, the customers, everything – is there because it perfectly harmonizes with the thoughts and beliefs on which you have focused up to now.

This may be hard for you to hear.

No one likes to think he is to "blame" if the things in his life are not as he would like. But it is not about assigning blame; it is about using a scientific law consciously so that you can improve your circumstances.

If you turn on a burner on your stove, and then put your hand on the burner, you will get burned. This is not because the stove was "out to get you" or it "just didn't work for you" to try that. Rather, it happened because it is the nature of electricity to flow where it is given outlet, and to radiate heat when channeled through a burner. To avoid getting burned, you simply get in harmony with this law of physics and avoid putting your hand on a hot burner. Children learn this instantly if they violate it!

Let's take this analogy one step further. Let's say you have an electric stove, and you decide to use it to heat your house instead of to cook with – so you move it into the living room. When the heat is inadequate, or is too focused in one room, or the room is unattractive because you have put a stove in the middle of it, are any of those things the fault of the stove? No!

These undesirable consequences are simply a result of your improperly using the laws of heating (and aesthetics!). And they can be changed by harmonizing with the proper laws instead.

This rather silly analogy explains why an entrepreneur can notice another business owner doing something that works well for that person, but when he applies it in his own business, it fails miserably. *The entrepreneur was not in harmony with the essence of – or vision behind – the strategy, so he will not enjoy the same results.*

It is easy to observe someone who is successful and then think deductively, trying to trace their success back to the specific steps that led them there. But this is doing things backward! Without having the vision *first*, and then taking actions that are in harmony with that vision to move in the direction of its manifestation, you will ever truly understand, or be able to replicate, that person's success.

Stephen Covey called this "beginning with the end in mind."

Think for a moment about the aspects of your business that are not pleasing to you. Perhaps you don't have enough money, or enough clients, or you are overwhelmed by the details (what I call "administrivia") of the business. Maybe you are unhappy with your outdated computer, or your undersized office.

First, take in the principle that you have attracted these things because that is what you are in harmony with right now. They may have even fit you very well in the early stages of your business – but the time has come to step up a level, to grow, and to expand.

Now – immediately! – realize that in the very moment you notice this principle at work, you can begin to change what appears before you in your business by changing your thinking right now.

Ask yourself: "What would someone believe, think about and focus on who has your ideal number of clients, your ideal amount of income, and the perfectly organized, beautiful, functional office you desire?"

Take a moment with that question. Do you know the answer? If you don't know what the person would believe, think and focus on, do you know someone who would exemplify your ideal? Go at least a couple of notches above the next step for you.

For example, if your goal is to be a multi-millionaire business owner, and you are currently making $90,000 per year, you are making $90,000 because that is the vibration with which you are in harmony now. To step into the mid to high 6-figures in income, you will need to emulate someone who is making *at least* that much now. Perhaps you think about Oprah, or Donald Trump, or Richard Branson. What kind of an office would/do they have? How do they respond when presented with a restaurant bill that is twice what they expected? Do they complain, or simply say "it's only money, I'm so glad we had this time together!"?

Starting to change your thinking and beliefs so you can harmonize with a higher way of thinking and believing requires that you have a crystal clear picture of the person you want to become. If you know someone that you can be coached or mentored by, or can at least interview and get a perspective as to their thinking patterns and approach to life, do it! This cements the picture in your mind of what you want – and you actually absorb their thought patterns just by spending time with them.

Finally, when presented with the daily situations of your life – whether to your liking or not – challenge yourself to think, speak, decide and act like the person you want to be, not the person you have been in the past. This will put you instantly in harmony with your higher way of living and doing business – and once you align your new beliefs with your thoughts and the actions you take, you will be amazed how that simple shift begins to attract other dimensions of the picture that you did not even know were there.

18
Manifesting

When we hear the word "manifest" used as a verb, many people interpret it to mean "create" – as in bring forth out of nothing. But that is not its definition!

Webster's dictionary defines manifest as "to reveal or display." So to manifest your dream is to reveal something that already is. Doesn't that sound easier than creating from scratch?

Revealing (aka manifesting) your business is more about clearing out all the beliefs, thoughts, and paradigms that are blocking you from seeing it than it is about working hard to "create" something from nothing. Fears, doubts, and beliefs about money and life are programmed into you subconsciously (where there is no filter to accept or reject). All of these can obscure the majesty of your vision, as well as your own confidence that you really can attain it.

Manifesting also requires that you accept and believe, at a core level, that you are surrounded by an ever-creating Substance. This Substance has formed the earth, the planets, the galaxies, and you. And this same Substance is available to you now as you manifest your business, both initially and as it grows.

What a concept: the same force that created the Universe is available to you, like clay to the potter, to create your book, your coaching program, your event, your computer program, your new product, or whatever you desire to develop and sell to your customers!

By thinking of your business in this way - and by working with the vision, the energetic essence, and the formless aspect of what you want to create – you will find that manifesting requires less work, fewer steps, and less energy. You simply get in touch with your dream or desire, clear out your resistance and other blockages, and decide that you will have it. Then, the way for it to come into your experience appears – more easily and effortlessly than you thought possible.

Patience comes naturally. In fact, to be impatient is to express distrust with this infinite Substance and its timing! Once you decide to have something, and are open to receive it, it *will* come – but sometimes not in the form or the timeline you had expected (it is often even better than that!).

You can have anything you want. Anything! Most people are so afraid to even consider that they could be millionaires, that they could own their own business, or that they could be happy, that they never make the decision to do so. It then becomes a self-fulfilling prophecy that they never have these experiences.

Be part of the higher-thinking minority that knows you deserve more, and that is committed to "going for it" in your life and business. You will not be disappointed as the Universe lays out for you all of your stated desires, as though on a silver platter.

And it is all available to you right now.

19
Purpose

You have come into this life with a specific life's purpose to express and unfold. It has been with you since before you were born – and you knew that this life, these people and the environment of being on earth at this time would be the best playground in which to bring it forth.

You may have been seeking to clarify your purpose for years. Or perhaps you did not even consciously realize you had one. And some of you know with crystal clarity what it is.

Each of us has a purpose; but if you are called to Purposeful Entrepreneurship™, your purpose is ready to unfold in a big way, as your "life's work" in and through your business. It will likely take you into positions of leadership, influencing thousands or millions of people, and walking ahead as an example to many of what is possible for them.

You may think you are unworthy of this big vision, or may think, "Who am I to do this?" But if you do not act on this vision – not just in your work but in your life as a whole – you will feel unfulfilled, like something is missing in your life.

And just as importantly, by not stepping into your purpose you actually deny those you could help of the opportunity to benefit from your work. If you don't bring your message to them, they may never hear what they need to hear!

To discover your purpose, simply look at two things: first, what do you absolutely love to do, feel passionate about, and would do, even if you were never paid for it?

Second, what core life issues or problems have you mastered which you could help others master too? Put simply, your purpose was to overcome these challenges, and your life's work is to help people who have faced issues similar or identical to yours and to share what you have learned in going through it.

If you have not previously clarified your life purpose, you will need to do so to move forward in your business as a Purposeful Entrepreneur™. But even if you know what your purpose is, realize that the way in which it expresses will change over time. And the degree to which your activities are on purpose will vary periodically too.

You may have started your business with purpose, but somehow all the details, the growth plans, and the daily grind of running the business may have obscured it.

Now is the time to recommit to the purpose you know at your core, and to remove anything from your life and your business that keep you from fully expressing your purpose every day.

Another obstacle you may experience in identifying and continuing to express your purpose is listening to the inner voice that says you cannot make a living doing that which your purpose directs you to do, that it is impractical, or that it would be foolish to acknowledge it.

The point is not whether you can "make a living" from your purpose; instead, think of your task while on earth to simply identify that core purpose and express it in all aspects of your life. Your relationships, lifestyle, career or business choice, educational course of study, hobbies, and even your spiritual path and religious beliefs, if any, should be expressions of the purpose that is central to your life.

Instead of "making a living," it is more a matter of "living your making." Every breath you take, every word you speak, every action you take... all are tied to your purpose. They may be an expression of it or a cry for its healing. But they are connected nonetheless.

Ideally, your life purpose will express as your life's work, and that life's work for those of you reading this book is your business, your products, your services and the customers you serve.

Dare to peer into your soul and ponder your deepest passions and your deepest wounds... together they form the essence of your life purpose, where your fulfillment and your contribution lie.

20

Passion

Most entrepreneurs begin their business with a sense of passion, excited about the freedom and other benefits that they expect owning their own business will provide. But even when learning the first few steps of the launch process, it is not uncommon to become overwhelmed and to lose that initial passion.

It is important that the passion truly flow from your purpose, and a genuine desire to serve – versus a raw drive for money or to get away from a boss with whom you did not get along. Think of your passion as the fuel for your vision, and you will realize its critical importance in starting and growing a Purposeful Entrepreneur™ enterprise.

Leverage its power when things get tough, when you have a disappointing result to a marketing campaign or a sales call. In fact, I recommend you make a list of all of the emotional and lifestyle benefits you believe the business will give you, as you are starting it. Reviewing this list in challenging times can retrieve your passion and help you remember why it is worthwhile to walk through the current challenge.

As a business grows, the infrastructure of the business becomes more complex – exponentially so as staff and product or service offerings are added, along with new business systems – and the initial passion you felt can give way to frustration.

So how to you recapture it once it has waned?

Simply admitting the need to do so is a principal first step. Instead, too many entrepreneurs (as well as employees!) simply press on, doing what is needed, hoping the passion will return in time – but it will not unless you notice that it has diminished. Repressing the loss of passion will lead to illness, unhappiness, and discord if left unchecked.

The frustration, stress, even despair that comes from seeing the passion drain out of the business is designed to be your doorway back into your heart, into the wiser part of you that knows what you are here to do – and how to regain that passion. When it seems masked, or it appears that you must simply continue on your current course because no one else can step in to help you, STOP.

Realize that you MUST have passion to fulfill your purpose.

Then, close your eyes, let the current issues that have been dis-tracting you float away for a few minutes, and breathe deeply. Tune into your heart, notice the fullness and softness you feel there. This is the essence of your purpose, still there, just pushed aside lately. After a few calming breaths, simply ask your wiser self, what needs to change for my passion to return? And listen for the answer.

Often, the answer will be to delegate something you are doing that you do not love doing, or to let go of a project that is more of a "have-to" than a "want-to". Or it may be something very illogical, like returning to a hobby or a creative practice you used to do. For me, it was singing – my recent re-awakening to my purpose came as I said yes to singing more often, just for myself many times, but doing it on a regular basis. I found that somehow that tapped me into my energy system, grounded me, and allowed me to access creativity and flow that was not there when I ignored my musical gift.

I cannot predict what your inner self will say – but I do know that it is wise beyond measure, and that if you listen and act on its wisdom, you will find your passion returning in no time. Just be willing to let go of what is not working to embrace your revived sense of passion. And work will become fun once again!

21
Profits

A business, by definition, generates profits. The first and most commonly understood kind of profit is "financial profit," meaning a positive cash flow. To have maximum impact in the world, a Purposeful Entrepreneur™ business should be as profitable as possible, generating as high of revenues as are possible. Why? Because money is our means of exchanging energy and value – and the more you have, the more you attract into your business, the more people you can serve, the more products you can develop and launch, and the bigger transformational contribution you can make.

But to be profitable means more than simply having money left over after business expenses are paid (though that is important too!).

The second kind of profit is "energy profit." If you are struggling to pay the bills, or operating at a financial loss in your business, the answer is not *only* to generate more sales or cut expenses (in fact the latter may hinder your progress if it fosters a constrictive energetic vibration within your business!). Lack of profit symbolizes an energy deficit within you. That is, it is indicating you are giving out more than you are receiving in return. If you start giving to yourself more, opening to receive more by blocking out time for recreation, relaxation and play, that energy surplus will begin to materialize in the finances of your business too.

The path of the Purposeful Entrepreneur™ requires that you cultivate the perfect balance between giving and receiving, yin and yang, inhale and exhale. If you are naturally driven and achievement-oriented (as most entrepreneurs are), your primary lesson will be to learn to receive, to relax, to set healthy personal boundaries between personal and business life. Mastering the principles of good financial management of your business will be relatively easy for you, even if you have not done it before. What is more difficult is avoiding the temptation to continue to work harder instead of smarter.

It really is possible to work easier (less hours) and earn more money! But it will require shifts in both your approach and your mental paradigm.

If, on the other hand, your natural tendency is to go with the flow, let things unfold, and play as much as you can, then your primary lesson as an entrepreneur will be to develop a healthy amount of structure within which your business can grow. For some entrepreneurs of this type, that means surrounding yourself with assistants and staff that can develop and maintain the structure, freeing you to do the creative work you love!

The third kind of profit is "lifestyle profit." What other kinds of profits does your business yield to you besides money? Profit is defined in the dictionary as "an advantage; a benefit." For many entrepreneurs, such benefits as lifestyle freedom, the potential for unlimited income, improved balance between work and play/personal time, and perhaps the flexibility of working from home are other benefits they receive from owning a business. If you have started your business and you are enjoying these experiences, you have "lifestyle profit."

A final kind of profit is "psychic profit." No, I'm not talking just about accessing psychic gifts (though you may do so). This kind of profit refers to the inherent fulfillment, satisfaction, and sense of greater contribution you experience as a Purposeful Entrepreneur™. Are you enjoying an abundance of these emotions, even after several years in business? If you are not, you likely are also lacking energetic profit now, as they are tied together. Returning the energetic balance and recommitting to your purpose will increase your psychic profit too.

What you must remember here is that while it is important to wisely manage your business income – including using skilled experts to help you – to be profitable, the financial profit is simply a reflection of the other three kinds of profits too.

22

Working with staff

To grow your business, you will likely need to bring on from one to many staff to help you. The best way to determine what tasks to delegate to them is to use the wisdom of my colleague John Assaraf: "Hire people who play at what you have to work at."

Your roles within your growing business should be those that you love, that come easily to you, and that truly use your genius, your strengths, and your creative gifts. Everything else should be delegated.

Usually you will recognize the need to delegate before you appear to have the funds available to pay for staff. The unenlightened response to this dilemma – being way too busy doing things that do not come easily to you but must be done – is to continue "doing your best" until that magical day when the money is there.

But the money may never come to one who embraces this way of thinking.

An important principle to remember is that "decision precedes supply." The very fact that you have the desire to bring people into your business to help you means the right people are already in your experience. (You may encounter them every day and not recognize their potential, until you decide you are ready to bring someone in to help you!) But you need to decide to fill the positions before you will recognize the right person for the job. Then, almost as if by magic, the supply appears.

In fact, by bringing a staff person on who can easily do what you struggle at doing – at a lower hourly rate than yours – brings immediate financial as well as energetic profit into your business. You can instantly start doing higher value tasks which add value (and likely income) to the business with your now freed-up time.

When you recognize a need for a staff person in your business, your next step is to list all of the traits, skills and expertise the ideal person for that role would possess, including their values, philosophy or other personality aspects. Then, check in with your inner self, sit quietly, and energetically attract them to you before taking any physical action. Imagine a coil of light emanating out from your heart to theirs, vibrating at the same level, and sharing a similar commitment to doing good in the world. Finally, take the physical action you are guided to take, whether that be to retain a recruiter, place an ad on Craigslist or a job board, or to call someone you know to either be – or find - a suitable candidate.

As you select the right person and negotiate their compensation, be open to creative arrangements in addition to the traditional employer/employee salary or wage model. Could they be a part-time contractor? Could they be compensated with a share of the revenues they generate that come into the program they are helping you develop and promote? Or a combination of both?

Once staff have come on board, you begin a journey together. Whether you sense tension between you and a staff member or incredible harmony, remember that it is all an expression of the vibration and energy between you. You may have attracted certain staff members to bring to light old family wounds or self-deprecating beliefs to be healed – and tension or conflict may be the gateway through which you come to terms with them. If you have done a degree of personal healing work, the new staff people you attract will be more in harmony with you and your vision than you were able to attract in the past.

To grow your business into the high six figures or seven figure in revenue, you will also need to bring people into your life to provide other support for you, such as helping with personal errands and other tasks that keep you from focusing on your genius. This will include housekeeping, cooking, grocery shopping, and the like. Each time you find yourself wanting to expand and grow, you will need to let go of everything that keeps you from doing so – and confront any beliefs you have that "no one can do it like I can."

Staff can free you or entrap you. The difference always comes down to personal healing and harmony, within you and within them.

23
Simultaneous implementation

We are taught to get everything ready, take careful aim, and then fire (i.e., launch). But the Purposeful Entrepreneur™ thinks in terms of "ready, fire, aim." Gather the basic information and determine the basic outline, then launch and test it. Plan to "aim" – to refine and perfect – *after* you have initial sales in the door. Fund your production with the initial sales (so-called "bootstrapping") instead of waiting until you have the funding or seed money to launch. This is the only way you will manifest in a massive way, accomplish many things simultaneously, and "burst onto the scene" of your marketplace, becoming a key player in days or weeks instead of months or years.

Perhaps the biggest barrier to growth for new entrepreneurs is taking a linear approach to their business. That is, they have one product idea, and build its prototype, its marketing plan, its revenue plan, and its customer target profile – and then implement that one product. Only after that product has been launched do they start on product number two or a service related to product number one... and as a result, growth is incremental rather than explosive.

If you are like the entrepreneurs I know, you are constantly coming up with new ideas – too many to implement. You may try to capture them in an idea journal, planning to implement at some future time. Or you may simply let them pass, knowing you are already too busy with what you are already working on. Unknowingly, you may be letting millions of dollars pass you by simply because you cannot implement more than one idea at a time. (And then you wonder why you become frustrated at not earning as much as you want to... right?)

Imagine what would be possible if you could implement four, five or six product ideas, businesses, or services at one time? "But," you say, "that would mean four times the cost, four times the headaches, four times the overhead – and I don't have it!"

If the desire is there, the means for its achievement is also there. Instead of thinking about what you *don't* have or *can't* do, ponder this: "What would need to happen for me to implement several of my ideas simultaneously?"

This power question will refocus your mind on possibilities, new rules that can turn the old ones on their head, ways it *can* happen instead of all the reasons it cannot.

Once you have the ideas in mind, you will first want to sort them based on which carries the most passion and joy for you, as well as on which will create the greatest return on investment, now and in the future, for you and your business. (And of course, they must all be in line with your life purpose, even if they represent new areas of business for you.)

Many of my colleagues and I have incorporated this philosophy into our business expansion. And the results are nothing short of remarkable. One woman used this approach over 6 months, consistently applying a proven business template, and launched more than 230 successful businesses in multiple industries in that time – while other entrepreneurs were struggling just to make one work!

The key is opening your mind to the simultaneous implementation approach as a legitimate one – and then taking the action that you are guided to take to attract like-minded partners or staff, creatively tapping into needed money and other resources, and daring to act boldly when others are tip-toeing tentatively.

24

Success

───────

Success is an illusion – if you view it as residing somewhere in your future and not in the now moment.

Its dictionary definition is "the achievement of something desired, intended or attempted." Most people read this to mean the moment of accomplishment, the completion of a project, the manifestation of a dreamed-of experience.

What if instead you read this to mean bring the *quality* of success – as you define it – into every moment of your waking life? You have identified your desires and stated your intentions for your business. If your definition of success cannot be brought into every moment, it will forever elude you.

Some high-achievers have a lengthy definition of success, down to the details of their body fat percentage, their portfolio value, their business' gross and net income as well as value/equity, the home they live in, the spouse they are married to and their annual travel agenda. Even when these people realize the items on this long list, the feeling of success eludes them – and they typically just make a new list of higher goals hoping that will yield them the experience they desire. And it is an endless cycle of disappointment.

By contrast, a simple definition of success such as "I bring joy to every moment" or "I experience everything in my life fully" can make every moment a success. The achievements along the way simply become icing on the cake, instead of the cake itself! This gives way to a kind of detachment from the results that paradoxically leads to better results that one gets when intently attached to things happening at a certain time and in a certain way.

Another danger of defining success in a way that requires certain achievements or events to precede it, given our tendency to think in opposites, is this: if you cannot say you are a success now, in this moment, then subconsciously you may be telling yourself you are a failure. And that will not empower you to apply your best thinking and your best skills toward your goals.

Take a moment now to articulate the qualities that represent success to you — qualities within you, qualities of your life experience, and qualities of your business interactions. Now, success becomes a matter of degree rather than something that you are or are not experiencing. Perhaps you can look back on yesterday and see that you embodied those qualities in a conversation or setting in which previously you were unable to do so — and that is progress!

By viewing success as a quality, not an end result, you are building a foundation for even more success tomorrow — and the momentum carries you forward to the life of your dreams.

25

Winning

Purposeful Entrepreneurs strive for a win-win-win in every transaction. If only you win, but your customer doesn't, it is not a true win. Unethical practices, unfair prices, diluting a product and charging more, and other similar actions are examples of this. And they always catch up with the person.

On the other hand, if your customer wins but you don't, you will likely be out of business soon! For example, your customer gets something for nothing, you discount below your cost, or you otherwise over-give and it is detrimental to your profitability or your product quality.

The ideal transaction will benefit you, the business owner, in the form of profit and the satisfaction of making a contribution and helping someone else. It will also benefit your customer, in that they get what they want, at a fair price, and with high quality. And it will also carry a third benefit, whether to your staff, to the people that will be impacted by your customer's use of it, or otherwise. This is a win-win-win result.

For example, when students enroll in my coach training programs, we receive their tuition investment and the satisfaction of knowing we have contributed to their improving their life. They win in that they have the opportunity to learn a new trade, and they get high value training at a reasonable cost. And the clients they will ultimately serve win too, both by the quality of their coaching skills and knowledge and by using the forms, templates and other materials we have delivered to help them clarify and achieve their goals.

Wallace Wattles expressed this in his powerful book, *The Science of Getting Rich,* as the principle of "more life to all, less to none." That is, "Give every person more in use value than you take from him in cash value. Then, you are adding to the life of the world with every business transaction." If the net result of a transaction is a loss to anyone, it will not lead to enhanced life.

To embrace this notion of winning – win-win-win instead of just a single win – we must set aside the competitive mindset of our culture, which says only one party can win. In the ideal transaction realm, *everyone* wins.

Notice where you may have been trying to win at the expense of others in your business. How could you create a bigger win for your customers and your market at large through one simple gesture or initiative?

The essence of Purposeful Entrepreneurship™ is expressing life for the benefit of all. You can start doing that today.

26

Congruence

N othing is more important to the rapid growth of your company than having congruence between your purpose and each aspect of the business. When two things are congruent, they are perfectly aligned, so that there is no dissonance between them.

Imagine the gears of an engine, which must fit perfectly, tongue into groove, and rotate in perfect harmony in order to power the motor. If a small particle gets between them, wearing one down more than the other, it will create friction. That friction means the gears must work harder to do the same task, grinding as they do so - and if not repaired, will ultimately break down.

Your business and its purpose are like the gears: they must align perfectly, with nothing interfering with them, to fuel the engine of your growth.

Obviously, the best time to make an adjustment is when the obstacle first appears, and simply removing it will prevent the uneven wear and friction that would later result. Is there any area in your business now that feels less enjoyable than it used to? Or where sales are diminishing where once they were growing?

Those are examples of the particle that can impair the operation and growth of your enterprise. What would you need to do or be to remove this obstacle now and restore the free flow of energy, income and creativity?

The sooner you can recognize the entrance of the "particle," the easier the change will be. But instead, most of us press on, telling ourselves we are just tired today, or we ate too much last night – that it will be more fun and more profitable next time.

But it won't – *if* a particle of dissonance has in fact entered into your business.

When you hear two discordant tones on a piano or violin, you wince – it is painful! Learn to hear your inner voice's language just as clearly. That wince is telling you to change who you are being, what you are believing, or how you are acting to restore the harmony.

One way of measuring the congruence in your business is to do a daily evaluation of your results and progress vis-à-vis the vision you have for your business when it is finished. Did today's (and this week's, this month's and this quarter's) initiatives, decisions and actions further your purpose toward your vision (congruence)? Or did they distract you and take you further away (dissonance)?

Seek the congruence – and the vision will unfold effortlessly.

27
Healing presence

Many of you reading this book are coaches, consultants, authors, speakers, trainers, and healers, directly involved in helping people heal or better their life in a specific area. But all entrepreneurs begin their businesses as healers and visionaries, whether they recognize it or not!

The person who wants to start an auto repair shop that provides outstanding customer service, an exceptionally pleasant waiting room and the highest quality repairs is healing by offsetting those that may be operating with a priority on getting instead of giving, shoddy work standards and unreliable repairs.

If everything is energy, then every interaction you have with a staff member, with a customer, or even with a project on which you are working, has an energetic consequence. The question is, are those consequences healing or damaging?

Eastern philosophies refer to this as karma: "Through the law of karma, the effects of all deeds actively create past, present, and future experiences, thus making one responsible for one's own life, and the pain and joy it brings to him/her and others." (www. wikipedia.org)

One of the roles of a healer is to see what the client or patient cannot see for him/herself. This information may be beliefs, causes behind behavior, or even auras or inner "stories" or conditions of which the person is unaware. Simply being willing to see the perfection of a person, be objective, and share the impressions that come is sacred work. And it often results in transformation.

Physicians take the Hippocratic oath to do no harm. As entrepreneurs, we would be well served to adopt a similar oath. In all our business, even in the midst of conflict, to do no harm. In all of our products and services, set the intention to do no harm, only good. We thereby add to the life on the planet, creating a positive karma through our actions. This also transforms our work into what the Buddhists called "right livelihood," one of the Noble Eightfold Path that leads to enlightenment, to deliverance from suffering.

Have you ever considered what the healing effects might be to your customers and others who deal with you and your business? This goes beyond emotional benefits to the widespread (perhaps global) contribution your business is making, each and every day.

Once you know what those healing effects are, you can leverage them by giving a percentage of your sales for a period of time to a related cause, foundation or organization, thereby building further goodwill with your customers and in your community.

Don't overlook the healing role you may be playing in the world. Your work is vitally important, and it is having far-reaching effects, the breath of which you may never know.

28
Boundaries and balance

Perhaps the biggest test of the Purposeful Entrepreneur's sanity is the never-ending stream of information and "to-do's" that bombards us every day, both regarding business and personal issues.

In the Industrial Age, it was easy to set boundaries between work and home: you simply walked out the factory door! You didn't take work home with you or think about work during dinner or while watching evening television. You took vacations (without Blackberries and laptops!) and you collected your paychecks regularly.

In the Knowledge Age, by contrast, your work is done with your mind, so it can follow you wherever you go – especially when you own your own business! And on top of that, many coaches and other service business owners work from home, so their laptop is just a few steps away at any time of day. And it is easy to let client preferences dictate the time you coach them – so that before you know it, your personal time is gone. Fewer people take vacations now than ever – but you can be an exception to that! (Ideally, your business should run without you anyway...)

I first learned the boundary-setting method I use now from Ken and Marjorie Blanchard (Ken is the author of *The One-Minute Man-*

ager). Each year, they sit down and plan out their *vacations first* for the year, and then the business commitments are scheduled around them. That is the exact opposite of what most people do!

Just as you should pay yourself first (through savings and tithing) when your income comes in, you should pay yourself first when it comes to time. Don't leave yourself with the "scraps" of what time is left after you fulfill everyone else's demands – there will soon be nothing left for you.

A happy balance between work and play results from healthy boundaries. And healthy boundaries are created by clarifying your desired lifestyle first, then determining how you will organize your time second.

For example, if you want to work four days per week, with Friday being a self-care day and/or the beginning of a regular three-day weekend, block those out now! If you want to take six or eight weeks of vacation, block those out at the beginning of the year. (I use a large erasable year-at-a-glance calendar for this.)

Then, determine how you will allocate those four days. Perhaps two days will be for providing your service (coaching, speaking, writing, etc.), one day will be devoted to marketing and one day to practice management. It is your call!

Be sure to invest some of your time and attention in your personal relationships too! Most people's goals and scheduled events are 70 percent business, 30 percent personal. Determine whether you want that to be different for you – and chart your course accordingly.

Human beings in today's culture seem to aspire to a mechanistic approach to life, working as long as they physically can... and then (too often) breaking down. But we are an organism, not a mechanism! We need breaks, we have cycles... and we can't be equally productive in every moment. Schedule in a Self-Care Day weekly, and honor your own body's urgings to take breaks, move and stretch. Your business will thrive when you do!

It is not difficult to have healthy boundaries and a balanced life – but the key is to outline and visualize your desired lifestyle first, and business second. Right priorities lead to right results. And you'll be more content too!

29
Attracting

You irresistibly draw into your business and life that which matches the intentions you set. You may have heard this called the Law of Attraction.

Before you become aware of this, you do it unconsciously. Your results may appear to be random or arbitrary when you use the Law unconsciously. We call this Unconscious Attraction.

Awareness that your intentions determine your actions and results is the first step to conscious attracting. What intentions would you have set (perhaps without knowing you did) in order to obtain the results you now have? What beliefs, thoughts and emotions would, by definition, have to underlie them?

For example, if you are attracting an abundance of money, the underlying intentions would be that there is plenty of money, that you can have it, and that you are ready to receive it now.

With awareness you can then begin to consciously set intentions that will logically lead to the improved results and greater life and business you want. You have taken responsibility for your results by doing this, and you can begin Conscious Attraction. (You can even take this further by consciously magnetizing someone or something to you, with the knowledge that they are already within your experience, awaiting your becoming aware of them.)

What we now call the Law of Attraction is simply a contemporary way of expressing Albert Einstein's theory that for every action, there is an equal reaction. For every intention, there is a result. For every desire, there is a supply.

Once you understand this Law, you can focus on the actual cause of the effects you see, rather than trying to change the effects themselves. For instance, if you notice an increase in conflict between you and your business partner, the solution is not to try to change them, or even to reduce the conflict directly. Rather, the answer is to ask yourself what the conflict is reflecting from within you. What beliefs or thoughts have you been holding that are manifesting as this conflict? And what would you have to believe for the conflict to go away? Once you make the internal shift, the external differences of opinion will dissolve.

The Law of Attraction is both neutral and consistent. It does not favor some and reject others; it acts equally on each person's dominant thoughts and intentions. If you are not receiving what you say you want, it may be because you are not energetically in harmony with it so that the mold of your intention can attract the substance of its physical reality.

When you set an intention that is much bigger or different than what you are currently experiencing, you will feel excited when you consider the possibility. But then you may, like many people, inadvertently focus your attention back on what you are experiencing now – which you *don't* want. That simply perpetuates more of what you have.

Be sure to keep your eye on the thing you want, not on what you don't want, in order to attract it.

30
Allowing

It is difficult to turn away from the societal programming that says you must work harder to obtain more, that urges you to "go for it!". In fact, once you begin building a business around your purpose, you will be required to let in more in order to have more. Sounds paradoxical, doesn't it?

Here is a simple metaphor. Let's say you ask your son to play catch, and you both go outside with the ball. You throw the ball to him and he catches it. He throws it back to you but your hands are closed. The ball is still there, but there is nowhere for it to go but rolling down the street.

If you set your intentions, focus on them, and *really* want them to occur, but your hands are closed when the Infinite Supply brings the results to you, then you cannot receive the good you desire.

Remove the stigma in your mind that says it is "bad" to simply "do nothing." As an entrepreneur, you must have time to renew and refresh yourself, to recharge your personal batteries so that you can once again give out to your customers, your clients, your staff and your business. This is the essence of the receptive, or Divine Feminine/yin energy which characterizes the Purposeful Entrepreneur Era.

To truly renew yourself, you need to unplug from your phone, email, and all work tasks for 24 hours (consecutively!) each week. Do something you love to do, go for a drive or a hike in the woods – or a walk along the beach. Learn a new hobby or go to the spa. It is your time, but it needs to be entirely non-work activity to be a Renewal Day.

Then, you can come back to your business with a fresh perspective and a greater sense of receptivity to what is longing to unfold through you.

Achievement-oriented entrepreneurs (and as we will see in the next meditation, that means most of us) need more rest and renewal time than most! It is as though we are on turbo-charge all the time we are working, burning through more fuel than we would if we were working in a 9 to 5 job for someone else.

What would your Renewal Day look like if you relaxed and played with as much zest as you work?

If you are working toward a goal and you find yourself forcing and pushing and struggling to "make it happen" – relax. Let go, and notice that you are resisting your experience. Resistance and allowing are opposites. You cannot create space for the good you desire if you are resisting and attempting to "push the river".

Consciously create space in your life, and you will find more customers, money and resources flowing to you. Creating space may take the form of cleaning out a closet, organizing your computer files, or uncluttering your mind of distractions that could be handled by an assistant. But each of these actions will create a vacuum – and you will notice something much more to your liking filling that space once it is clear.

Allow your good – and your business will thrive.

31
Achievement

It has long been acknowledged that successful entrepreneurs have what Dr. David McClelland called the "achievement orientation." That is, they are intrinsically motivated by the opportunity to take consistent, regular action toward an important goal.

You may have noticed this from your earliest memory, on the playground and in the classroom, among your siblings and with your friends. Entrepreneurship simply gives you a positive way to channel that achievement orientation into a business that does good in the world.

However, the shadow side of achievement is over-achievement, workaholism, and burnout. If you allow yourself to be a slave to your achievement orientation, it will endanger your health and lead to dis-illusionment in your work and business. Some entrepreneurs seek to temper this drive to achieve with alcohol, drugs, or other addictions. This too is a futile path.

Notice and appreciate your ability to think quickly, to be decisive, to turn your random thoughts into profitable business ventures. These are among your best qualities!

The biggest challenge for the achiever is to ask for help.

And it critical to your ultimate success for you to do so. Your achievement orientation will draw others to you, since it allows you to accomplish much in a way others will want to emulate. Continually ask yourself if what you are doing now is tapping into your genius and allowing you to bring your best skills to the table – those that no one else can bring.

Do those things – and delegate or systematize everything else.

Pause to celebrate your achievements when they occur. Don't fall into the trap of setting higher and higher goals, seeking the adrenalin rush of the hunt – but avoiding the calm contentment of completion. You deserve it!

Don't let others discourage you from using the drive you have to achieve great things; that is why you are on the planet at this time. They may not understand it, they may be jealous of it, they may even ridicule you. But your calling is your calling – no one else's. And you have been given this drive to help you fulfill it.

Use your achievement orientation wisely, and it will spur you on to truly remarkable accomplishments.

32
Lifelong learning

Nothing ever stands still. You, and everything in your environment are constantly moving forward or moving backward — there is no in between.

Resting on your laurels just won't cut it.

No matter how much you have accomplished, how highly skilled you are, or how successful you have become, you must continue learning in order to grow — or even maintain - that success.

When was the last time you learned something new? Not just read something interesting in the morning paper... I mean learned a new skill or language, gained a new area of expertise, or discovered and practiced a new marketing or business development technique? What about spiritual growth and learning — have you sought out opportunities to go deeper and enhance your spiritual wisdom recently?

For most people, this does not mean going back to school for several years and investing tens (or hundreds) of thousands of dollars. In today's fast paced world, the amount of information in the world doubles every 12 to 18 months. There is no way you can keep up with everything!

But if you can be the one that stays most current about your specific niche area and be the "go-to" person for your customers and clients, you will never lack for new business!

Staying current for your customers (your tribe) is not the primary reason to continue learning, however. The primary benefit is for you. Recent studies of brain physiology and aging have found that keeping the mind active – and especially stretching it to learn new things – keep you young and vibrant much longer.

Devote at least one hour each day to learning, whether you spend that time reading a book or report, listening to an mp3 or audio CD, viewing a video on a topic of interest to you and your work, or spending time with a coach or mentor. Branch out! Learn a marketing tactic one day, a meditation technique the next, and how to write an ebook or a business plan or a poem the next. Keep challenging yourself to stretch beyond your industry, beyond what is comfortable, beyond what you have always done.

So your learning will benefit your clients and yourself – but it also sends the Universe a message that says you are committed to being the best in your field, and that you deserve to take one hour of the time you devote to your work every day to give back to yourself. This is a huge affirmation of your self-worth and your readiness to receive more in your life – to move to the next level of abundance, income and balance.

Stretch your mental muscle today – and begin a practice of life-long learning. You will be glad you did – and you may just find that new product, program and business improvement ideas come from doing so too!

33

Customer service

Your customers are a reflection of you. And how you treat them directly reflects how treat yourself – and therefore how you view yourself. Observe your behavior with your customers and clients objectively, as though you were witnessing it from above. What do you notice? Does it make you want to be one of your own customers

The original meaning of the phrase "to serve" means "to treat as he deserves." And I would add, to treat as *you* deserve. If you treated every customer or client the way you would like to be treated, what would change? This is the Golden Rule in action.

One of my colleagues recently developed a high-end intensive one-on-one coaching program for a client. To make it of maximum value, she asked herself what *she* would want if she were looking for coaching. And she included all of those ingredients in this program, charging a six-figure fee for it!

The value of your customer is not determined by the present transaction you are doing with them. Instead, think of the *lifetime value* of that client. If they continued to work with you both now and over the next 20 years, how much money would they spend with you?

What kind of a relationship would they want to have with you that would keep them coming back for more?

Once you embody that sense of honor, respect and caring that accompanies this perspective, you then want to convey it to all of the people who touch your clients or customers in your business. Ideally, everyone from the receptionist or virtual assistant to the sales representatives, program managers, division vice presidents, manufacturing workers, bookkeepers, financial managers – *everyone* in the business – will treat the customers as people of great value.

As a Purposeful Entrepreneur™, you know this perspective is not only about how much money the person will spend with you as a customer; it is about who they are as a person. Everyone deserves to be here, and everyone has their own mission and purpose to fulfill. Your path and theirs have intersected for a reason – even if it seems to be only about their purchasing a widget from you. In some small (or large) way, you will impact their life. Will it be for the better or for the worse? Will you help them bring forth a new part of them that is ready to emerge, or will you bring to light an area of conflict or pain for healing? In either case, your dealings with them are truly service, not just business.

When someone is rude to you, or blames you for something you did not do – or even involves you in legal action – notice what is being reflected about you in the situation. It is difficult not to point the finger of blame and play the victim in a situation like this. But every time we point one finger to another, our other fingers are pointing back at us. Something is there within you to be healed or transformed or upleveled – and this situation is the perfect catalyst for that healing, if you will choose to view it that way.

Consider the way you would interact with someone you admire - a coach, mentor or other role model – and treat your customers or clients with the same respect. When they feel cherished, honored and heard, they will be irresistibly drawn to you to experience that again. Far too few people take the time to simply validate another person for who they are – and as a business owner, you have the opportunity to do that every day.

Systems

Notice what emotional reaction you have to the word "systems." Does it connote restriction or freedom for you?

In fact, you already have systems of organization in your business. They may be conscious or unconscious – but they are there. A system is defined simply as "an orderly pattern or arrangement," or "a group of elements that interact and function together as a whole."

Energetically, there are two important principles to keep in mind regarding systems in your business. First, by taking the action of organizing the disparate and disorganized elements within your business into one or more cohesive systems, you literally release a *huge* amount of energy for expansion and growth. When order is lacking, energy leeches out through every "hole" in the organizational structure and drags the vibration of the business and its staff down. No one wants to spend inordinate amounts of time trying to find misplaced or misfiled items, to create policies where no policy exists, or to get permission to act on something that is relatively routine. Systems change all of that.

The second important principle is that systems can be fundamentally changed by the people who interact with them. For example, if you create a system for writing and publishing an e-book, customer A may choose to apply *most* of your system and then add a couple of elements of their own – and it is suddenly a different system. It may even create a different product, such as an audio book instead of a written book! If the next person applies customer A's system and then adds to it, it once again morphs.

When I wrote my very first book (no longer in print), its audience was primarily consumers. But I found it resonated with – and sold to – an unexpected audience in consumer fraud attorneys who had no updated resource to which to refer. What a delightful synchronicity!

If you have not yet systematized your business – including operations, finance, marketing, legal, staffing, and overall policies – then you are not having as much impact as you could in the world. Begin by observing what you do, and how you do it – and document (or have one of your staff document) each step. Devote one hour per day or one day per week to the project, and you will be amazed at how much more effective you will be, how bottlenecks will be unclogged and holes will be plugged.

Systems must be reviewed and revamped periodically to stay relevant and effective. What works in year one of your business will be inadequate in year five.

When you create or recreate a system, give yourself permission to ignore convention. Even if "everyone" does it a certain way, be willing to ask why! If an unconventional system – or even skipping steps in a proven system – seems more practical, more growth-producing or more logical for you, try it! Don't be afraid to turn the rules by which others operate – or by which you have operated up to now – on their head.

Marketing gurus such as Dan Kennedy encourage entrepreneurs to take a marketing system or strategy that works in a different industry and try it in your own. Remarkable results can follow!

35
Focusing

To focus is to create clarity around something. As you have clarified your purpose and your life's work, you have brought focus to what you do for your profession. But it is not something that is done once and for all!

The biggest issue with which I see entrepreneurs struggle is staying focused despite a myriad of distractions, both in the day's activities and in the bigger picture of fulfilling their purpose through their business. You just get your staffing the way you want it, and someone gets pregnant or their parent falls ill. Or just as your new software is released to the market, Microsoft changes the Windows platform and you have to go back to the drawing board to recreate it. Or perhaps what distracts you is as simple as the compulsive need to check email while in the midst of a big project, or someone who calls or stops by and asks if you've "Got a minute?" – and a half hour later, you get back to what you were working on.

Distractions are rampant, focus is at a premium.

Give yourself the gift of disciplined focus for at least three specified one-hour intervals during the day. (Most executives fail to have even one hour of focused time during their day!) Set your intention to accomplish three to five key tasks during each interval, set a timer for one hour, and allow no distractions. These Focus Hours will allow you to almost magically progress toward your priority goals, without making you feel constricted by too much structure.

If you find yourself being frequently distracted during the day, ask yourself what you are avoiding. Could that issue that just crossed your mind be taking your attention away from an important realization you were about to make, or an aha! moment on that new product design?

If you are not avoiding something, ask what you are afraid you will miss out on if you don't pay attention to the distraction. Fear of being left out or not knowing/having the latest and greatest widget can sabotage productivity when it prevents focus.

When you are in a sales conversation with a prospective customer, the person who can maintain the greatest focus on his desired result (seller or customer) is the one who will win the day (and the sale).

The root word for focus meant "fire" – so you literally remove the flame, the fuel, the fire from your work if you are constantly flitting here and there and not paying attention to one thing for the length of time needed. Studies have proven that multi-tasking (doing more than one thing at once) is counterproductive – people are at least 40 percent less productive when multitasking then when doing just one thing and concentrating on it.

To improve your focus, practice the old meditation technique of setting a timer for 5 minutes to start, and concentrate on breathing in to the count of 1, out to the count of 2, and do this until the timer goes off. Gradually increase the time until you can do this for 15 or 20 minutes or longer. You can also practice keeping your attention on an object such as a candle flame, the branch of a tree outside, or a

stone. It is amazing how exercising this muscle of focus in a deliberate way will help keep you focused in your work and business too.

36

Technology: servant or master?

Using technology in your business is a necessity. But do you use it or does it use you?

The word "technology" comes from the Greek root meaning "systematic treatment of an art, craft, or technique." However, over time it has evolved to mean both the application of science and the specific devices that mechanize processes or tasks.

In an earlier lesson, we discussed the principle that energy is freed when you systematize a process in your business. And that was the initial intent of technology! But for many entrepreneurs, technology has led to their feeling tethered to their business 24 hours a day – especially if they have not set healthy boundaries regarding their availability to others through these devices.

PDA's, laptops, cell phone, pagers, and now Ipods, Twitter, and Facebook has people scrambling to keep up with what's latest and greatest. Managing email, optimizing your web site, and staying abreast of the newest internet marketing practices can be a full-time job.

If technology overwhelms you at times, or you find yourself spending more and more of your life using it (when perhaps you would prefer to take your child to the park or get a massage), STOP! Technology is insidious, and can get an unyielding grip on you before you know it.

How could you take a break from the technology that is driving you, get a higher perspective on what is *really* important – and make needed changes?

Many entrepreneurs love variety in their life and work – and technology can become just another distraction to bring a sense of variety into your day. But is it *productive* to leave your email open all day while you work on other projects, jumping at a moment's notice when the next email comes in? Some companies are now experimenting with a "no email Friday" instead of casual Friday – with great results! Many entrepreneurs are testing the practice of checking email just once in the morning and once in the late afternoon, or having their assistant handle all email – verbally checking in with them regarding items they can't answer.

And what about your phone line – whether land line or cell phone: do you *have* to answer it, just because it rings? Check in with your intuition first and make a gut decision as to whether to answer it. Or designate specific hours to answer the phone, and certain hours when you are focused on writing, coaching or other projects within your business.

There is also something my friend Melanie Benson-Strick calls the "Bright Shiny Object Syndrome," by which you hear about or see a new device or system or product - and you "must" have it! Notice whether you are telling yourself that "if I just had a new _____ (computer, web site, webcam, client management system, etc.), THEN I would be successful." Or perhaps you have convinced yourself that by buying just this one more book/CD program, you will finally get the information you need to be successful.

I am all for learning and growth – we have a lesson on that in this book too! But when it comes right down to it, what you need to launch and grow your business is within you. Technology will help you manage and market that business, and will assist in efficiently handle communication with staff and customers. But if you let technology rule your life, it will drain the life force out of you and you will have little left to give to your customers or your business.

37
Coming from your heart

It is relatively easy to act and speak from your heart, with love,
when your business is new, and the passion runs hot. But one of
the gifts of owning a business is that you have embarked on a "path"
(the *tao* or the way) of entrepreneurship. That means at times it will
break open your heart, it will call forth your emotional wounds to be
healed – and it will invite you to help and serve others who have had
similar wounds. This, as we discovered earlier, is part of your purpose
and life's work.

What if you came from your heart in all you did? If you were no
longer afraid to face the feelings you have?

Our culture – and the business world at large – tends to discount
emotions and favor the intellect. Emotions are messy. They cannot be planned, scheduled and controlled – and so, the culture says,
handle them on your personal time.

And yet, beneath the text of every business interaction and transaction lies a subtext of emotion. People buy based on emotion, and
then justify the purchase based on logic.

Indeed, it is within your greatest wound where the healing for others – and your greatest gifts – lie. If you discount it, suppress it, or

engage in addictions or other sabotaging behavior to ignore it, it will still be there, patiently waiting for healing. And your work will not be as successful, as far-reaching, or as impactful as it can once you bring that wound out into the open.

I am not suggesting that you engage in deep emotional processing while trying to do business with a customer! But rather, that you be open to healing your past wounds, in a safe environment (coaching or counseling session, in-depth retreat, etc.) and that you then bring the wisdom and lessons of that healing into the work that you do.

One practice that can build your awareness in this area can be done just before you make a business call, take a coaching client call, or begin writing or working on a project:

Take a moment to close your eyes, take several deep, slow breaths, and relax. Then, consciously focus your attention on your heart, the area in the center of your chest that is your center of love and compassion. Visualize a connection between your heart and your mind, perhaps as a ray of light connecting them. Then, see your heart radiating out love, compassion and emotional connection with all the people that you meet or interact with, or in the project you are about to work on. See yourself actually thinking and speaking from your heart, not your mind. Then, as you open your eyes, keep your focus in that heart area as you do the task or have the interaction. Consciously be receptive to the messages and insights it offers. You will find yourself creating, speaking and acting from a much higher perspective than your human mind alone.

Coming from your heart also means that you pay attention to how you are *really* feeling in any given moment. Many men and women tend to suppress feelings that are inconvenient for what is going on in the moment. And in doing so, you may miss an important message from your heart about whether to proceed with a project, when and whether to contact someone, and what stories from your past are now ready to be healed.

Learn to heed your emotional wisdom as well as your intellectual wisdom, and you will multiply your success.

38
The void

Perhaps one of the scariest times for the entrepreneur is the time of emptiness, when sales slow-down, or you have lose your excitement about what you are doing. We call this "the void." What is important to understand is that it is a natural part of the cycle of life, and of business. If the trees never shed their leaves in autumn, they could not burst forth with new life and shiny green leaves in the spring.

It is not a question of whether you will experience the void – but when. The phase of emptiness occurs in any transition to the new. In fact, many successful entrepreneurs deliberately create the emptiness by cleaning out closets, letting staff members go, selling out slow-selling products, etc. so that they can make room for the new.

As a Purposeful Entrepreneur™, you are called to a big vision, a large-scale work in the world. You will need to become more in order to bring this vision into being. And in the process, your personality self will need to let go of certain ways of being, beliefs and behaviors – much like the snake sheds its skin – so that your higher self can more fully express.

It is tempting at such times to take any action, make any decision, do *anything* – just to restore the sense of stability and calm once more.

Don't do it.

Allow yourself to stay in the discomfort, to ask the questions of the heart that may emerge here, and to shed what is no longer working. These practices will enable the greatness within you to come forth.

Money will also ebb and flow in your life and business. Sometimes the bills will appear to exceed the supply; sometimes there will be more than enough. On some occasions, there will be just enough coming in to pay the bills, and on still others there may seem to be no flow at all. These four states have been called ebb, flow, calm and flat by Sanaya Roman in *Creating Money.* Notice which of these is most comfortable for you. It is easier for you to have just enough to pay the bills, such that you generate more bills once there is an excess?

Notice too that each of these four states is a natural part of the cycle of money. The challenge during the ebb cycle (more money going out than coming in) is to hold fast to your vision and desire, even though there may be no physical manifestation of it yet. As Sanaya Roman puts it, "Even if you are in debt, you may still have a large net worth; it just hasn't yet been converted into dollars." Incurring debt is actually a demonstration of others' belief in your future earning ability. Can you see it too? During the flow state, you may need to challenge yourself to keep inviting in more.

You are being invited to embrace the void, to honor the natural cycles of life, business and money – and to hold your beliefs, your vision and your sense of self firm despite any external shifts, even as you look for the lesson within the experience.

Who you are is much bigger than any circumstance. And every cycle is temporary.

Responsibility

In common use, the word "responsibility" has a sense of heaviness to it – the "musts" of life. Indeed, it is defined as "having a duty or obligation." But what if you simply thought of it as your "response-ability" – i.e., your ability to respond – to your life and business?

How present can you be each day? How proactive can you be in anticipating new customer needs, listening to your intuition, and seeing beneath the facial expression and words being spoken? How well can you quickly adapt to changes in your dreams and desires, changes in the market, and changes in technology? Your adaptability is part of your response-ability. And entrepreneurs have an edge because we can be nimble and respond quickly. Use it!

It is so much easier to blame others – our upbringing, the government, our spouse, or even the weather! – for what we dislike in our life. But in fact, every part of your life is there because you have manifested it through your thoughts and beliefs. Can you take responsibility for it all and appreciate that, whether it is pleasing or not, you are beholding your creation?

Only through assuming full response-ability for our life can we change it. As long as it is someone else's fault that our business hasn't grown faster, that we have too many bills, or that we don't have a specific talent to share, then it will be up to someone outside ourselves to remedy it.

And they usually won't do it.

Taking responsibility also means owning our part in an interaction – even if the other person was "mostly" to blame. Any conversation or interaction involves two people, and if it does not go well, the responsibility is shared. Are you able to go to someone with whom you have had an unpleasant interaction and say, "I don't feel good about how I responded to you in that conversation, can we try it again, and I'll work on listening more compassionately?" (Or whatever is called for given the topic and situation.) It takes courage to be response-able – but it pays off in enriched relationships as you are more authentic, more attuned to your own feelings and reactions – and willing to take action to make things right again. This is part of your role as an enlightened Purposeful Entrepreneur™. And your example will have a ripple effect that will go far beyond what you personally see.

To become more response-able, you will need to pay attention to any place in your life or business where you are shutting down – on any level. Is there just a little less life in your relationship with a key staff member? Do you feel ever so slightly less excitement about a task you have within your business? Noticing these early warning signs can help you determine whether to delegate, systematize, confront someone, or take other proactive action to maintain an optimum life flow. This careful noticing will pay huge dividends!

Compressing time

How long do you think it will take until your business is success-ful? What if you could cut that time in half, or reach that goal in one-tenth of the time you thought it would take?

Challenging the paradigm of time is another of the opportunities you have as a Purposeful Entrepreneur™. Quantum physics has turned old paradigms - about matter as well as time - on their head. Quantum leaps occur in a nanosecond... and all of a sudden everything is different.

What would happen if you could experience a quantum leap in your business right now?

The desire you have to launch a new product – or simply to start your business – has no time. It can only be in the "now," so the only delays to its manifestation are your own beliefs about how long it must take, your paradigm about what must precede it, or resistance to it coming to you now – that is, failure to step fully into the experi-ence as a present reality.

Look first at how long you think things "must" take. Notice that for our culture to function as a whole, it has adopted widespread beliefs that certain things take time – with larger things taking longer than smaller things.

But there is no size to the Universe.

You can go immediately from $100,000 in income to $1 million – if you can remove all of the internal barriers to it happening. You can achieve instant fame, instant success, instant sales – but you must let go of your programming about how it must be. Within your environment right now, there are opportunities you are not seeing. You cannot see them until you expand your perception of what is possible for you. And then they will "appear" to you. My mentor tells the story of having an opportunity to triple his income in his environment for two years – somewhere he walked by every day – but he did not notice it until he changed his belief about what he wanted, what he deserved, and what he could earn.

If you were already that 7-figure business owner, how would your life change? How would you think? What decisions would you make differently? What kind of help and support would you have in your life and business that you have not yet put in place? Start acting, thinking and speaking as that 7-figure business owner – and the physical reality of that *must* become your reality. Form follows thought.

The second barrier to compressing time is the order in which things "must" occur. Even within information marketing, we have been taught that your marketing pipeline must start with a free offering, then a low cost offering (less than $100), then one for several hundred dollars, and finally your "flagship" offering of a deluxe coaching program or package, for $1000, $10,000 or more.

This is linear thinking, and it must be smashed if you wish to experience a sudden and exponential jump – a quantum leap – in your level of income and/or success.

Quantum thinking says to go for your real desire first – don't "work up to it" with lesser offerings that do not hold the same level of pas-

sion as your flagship product. I did this as I launched PurposefulEn-
trepreneur.com. I realized that after sketching out a detailed marketing funnel with multiple levels, what I really wanted most was the
high-end coaching group and the live events that were at the bottom
of the funnel. Conventional wisdom said I should launch the lower
priced items first and wait a few months before launching the rest...
but I disregarded that and started first with the items that made my
heart sing. And the results were spectacular.

The third barrier to compressing time, resistance, is more subtle.
Its typical usage is to "oppose actively," to take a stand against something. When used in the context as a barrier to manifesting what
you desire, it often occurs beneath the surface – at the subconscious
level of your mind. Deep-seated beliefs and cultural messages cause
you to subconsciously resist what you consciously desire. And until
you can clarify what that belief is and change it, you are doomed
to repeat the same patterns in your business and life. If something
seems delayed in coming to you, or a business initiative is not garner-
ing the results you had expected, make the assumption that resistance has reared its head. Then ask yourself, "what must I be resisting
for this to be demonstrating less than desired results?" The answer
may surprise you.

41
Synchronicity

Planning, while helpful, is overrated.

It has been said that "Life is what happens while you are making other plans." And it does seem that as soon as you make plans for your business, they change. But happily, they often change for the better, with something unfolding that is superior to what you had envisioned.

This kind of "synchronicity" occurs more often when your intention is for the greater good, your vision is clear, and you are open to more than one pathway to its achievement.

Wikipedia defines the term this way: "Synchronicity is the experience of two or more events which are causally unrelated occurring together in a meaningful manner. In order to count as synchronicity, the events should be unlikely to occur together by chance." If you have ever had something unexpected happen to you, it was likely synchronicity.

Let's say you have identified a need for a media placement specialist to help you build visibility for a new product you are launching, but you have no contacts in that area. Just as you identify the need, you find yourself standing in line at the theater and overhear a conversation between two people. One is clearly a media buyer for a local television station. Is the fact that you are standing just feet from each other a "coincidence," or is it two events causally unrelated (you didn't set up a meeting with the person or set out to find them) that are occurring together, seemingly by chance?

Being open to synchronicity, noticing it when it happens, and even consciously seeking to attract it, are all practices of the path of Purposeful Entrepreneurship™. When you are living your purpose, consciously and purposefully creating your business as you go, other people, resources, money, and everything else you need will be irresistibly drawn to you. And one of the means through which this happens is by the principle of synchronicity.

As the size of our planet literally shrinks with technological access worldwide, these meaningful convergences of seemingly unrelated events becomes even more obvious. Recently, a variety of bee that has been traced back to the Great Barrier Reef of Australia has made its way to the U.S. and is consuming whole hives of bees here, affecting honey production, growth of plants and flowers, etc. Who could have anticipated that a DNA mutation in one country would affect the honey production in another?

Similarly, every thought that you put out into the Universe, every word you speak, every action you take has effects that are far-reaching – perhaps to the other side of the planet or beyond. The Buddhists call this karma. But regardless of what you call it, we must each be mindful of our mental powers to affect change. If it really matters how you treat that driver that just cut you off, and your exhibiting love and tolerance in that circumstance could in some way contribute to world peace, you may rethink your knee-jerk reaction to "get even with him."

Acknowledging this power means that whatever your desire or need, simply claiming it for yourself and for the greater good means that the forces of the Universe immediately go to work bringing it to you. So don't give up just because you don't see it in the next 5 minutes! One of my colleagues, Fabienne Fredrickson, refers to this as the "short order cook" syndrome. You go into a restaurant, place your order for a ham sandwich, and the waitress takes the order to the kitchen and the cook starts to prepare it. But you don't see her come back with your sandwich, so you change your mind and decide you'd rather have the fruit plate. So she goes back, changes the order, the cook stops making the sandwich and starts making the fruit plate. But it takes longer this time, because the cook had to change one thing and start the other.

Successful people make decisions quickly, and change them slowly. And, I might add, they are open to synchronicity too. Changing your mind simply delays your good in coming, and forecloses the happy coincidences of events that would otherwise occur to bring you what you want more quickly.

42

Competition

G ive up the notion of competition as a basis for success.
To compete with someone is "to be in rivalry with" them.
This is the model on which traditional business is founded. But it is
giving way to cooperation as the new model of Purposeful Entrepre-
neurship™. This new model is all about "working together toward a
common purpose or end." There is room for everyone in the Coop-
erative Model, but only room for a few in the Competitive Model.

If we truly live in an abundant universe, and everything we desire
can be achieved or obtained, then there can be no truth in competition. It says that if I win, you lose. If I get the contract, you don't.
But what if you decided there was a place for both of us — maybe in
the same piece of work! Unless we are open to helping each other
succeed, each of us using only our true strengths and bringing in
colleagues who have different and complementary strengths as well,
then no one truly wins.

Part of the reason for the 2008 collapse of the financial, real estate
and automobile manufacturing markets was because they have been
based on the Competitive Model — and it no longer works. Competition dictates that winning is the goal, and winning is to be done at

any cost. Raping our environmental resources, irresponsibly managing finances and violating investor trust are too high a price to pay for winning.

Thus the new model is being ushered in.

As a Purposeful Entrepreneur™, you bring a unique combination of gifts and talents to the marketplace that, if you "own" it, virtually eliminates any competition anyway. No one else can be you – and no one else can deliver your service or create your product in the unique way that you do.

In tribal groups of native people, each person was given a name that reflected this special calling and gift upon entering adulthood. What if, instead of looking for how to successfully compete and "win" business over others in our field, we looked instead for their individuality as well as our own, and found ways to leverage both? Business would change overnight.

Seek out ways to cooperate with peers – and even so-called competitors. Can you combine your talents and have the whole be bigger than the sum of the parts? Ultimately, it is cooperation that will save the day, allowing even more of each person's greatness to manifest.

43

Saying no

S uccess is more about saying no than saying yes.

While you must say "yes" to the initial calling within you to become an entrepreneur, you will be asked to say "no" more than "yes" many times along the way – if you are to achieve maximum results for yourself and your business.

Economist Vilfredo Pareto pioneered the Pareto Principle which says that 80 percent of your effects come from 20 percent of your causes. Applying that to business, 80 percent of your sales come from 20 percent of your clients, and conversely 80 percent of your customer service attention is spent with the most difficult 20 percent of your clients. Until you can say "no" to the 80 percent of your clients that are not your best clients, for example, you will continue to feel fragmented and scattered in your sales efforts.

As you develop more product and service offerings, 80 percent of your sales will come from 20 percent of them too. It takes strength (and a deep breath or two!) to make the decision to discontinue or sell off the other 80 percent of your offerings. But you will be glad you did as you see the complexity of your business decrease, and free up energetic space for new products as well.

When you are evaluating a business opportunity – be it a new client, a joint venture partnership, or a product you may resell – pay attention to both the logic and the intuitive hunches you get about the opportunity. And don't be afraid to say "no" when it just doesn't feel right. Though you will never know what heartache, time and expense you have saved by doing so, you can learn to trust your gut instinct.

When you are too busy, say "no" to clients that will require more support than normal. And say no to undercharging for your services too – it is when you are too busy that you should raise your fees!

Let your inner wisdom guide you even about what may appear to be enviable, high-profile opportunities to share your message. If your inner guidance says "no," be sure it is not a fear-based "no," but an insight cautioning you against proceeding in this way, with this person or company, or at this time – and say "no." Then, don't look back with regret over what might have been – stand firmly in your decision and know that an even greater opportunity is ahead.

Ambition

How ambitious are you? The self-employed are hard-wired to be ambitious, since its definition is "a strong desire to achieve something," and as we saw earlier, achievement orientation defines the successful entrepreneur.

But it can become a liability instead of an asset when the outward energy of ambition overrides the inward energy of allowing. Purposeful Entrepreneurs need a balance of both types of energy.

In the 1970's, social researchers predicted that within 20 years Americans would have so much leisure time that it would become a kind of "crisis of leisure."

Obviously, that has not happened.

Ambition and the endless quest to "do more with less" have taken us in just the opposite direction. If you feel like you are working harder than ever, you are! Americans work longer hours than people in every other country in the world except Japan. And entrepreneurs are particularly hard-hit – if you are like the typical first-year business owner, you will work 60 or more hours per week and actually have *less* family time (at first) than those who work for someone else.

Its Latin root means "eager or inordinate desire of honor" – so it is as though the ambitious are trying too hard to earn what will come naturally if they simply apply themselves patiently and consistently. The test for the Purposeful Entrepreneur™ is whether you can hold a big vision for your work, but not invest an inordinate amount of energy working hard to achieve it. Instead, taking action while staying open to synchronicity will yield the best results.

Notice, too, that by focusing on an ambitious drive toward the next goal, the next marketing campaign, the next income milestone – that you miss the present moment. Your business, your life, and your customers need you to be fully present NOW.

Purposeful Entrepreneurs™ must constantly walk the tightrope balancing ambition and drive with being here now, being receptive to their good, and allowing new creative ideas in.

One of the best ways to come back to the present moment – once you become aware that your ambition has taken you away from it – is to simply take a deep, slow breath (or several). Bring yourself mentally and physically back to the place you are sitting, the life you are living, the work you are here to do. If something has gotten you wound up emotionally, ask yourself: "Will this really matter a month or a year from now?" If not, then why are you giving it so much of your life energy now?

Tempering ambition and allowing will take you to more lasting success by far than a continual drive for more... which will wear you down physically and repel much of the good that wants to come to you.

Ego

Some have defined the ego as "Edging God Out." Though a healthy sense of self is needed to develop our individuality, it can limit our success if we rely solely on it in charting our business direction. The further we move along the path of our purpose, the more important it becomes to surrender the ego and sense of personal importance to the Higher Purpose moving in and through us.

Certainly it is satisfying to have people respond favorably to your work and the products you create. But if you are looking to your business and its success to provide you with a sense of self-esteem, you will never find it there. You must develop self-esteem and then express, from that place of fullness, through your business. To do otherwise is to be codependent on your business – and paradoxically, no matter how many best-selling books you have, how much money you make, or how large the crowds are at your workshops or other events, you will never feel you have "arrived" at that place of self-esteem until you bring it to the work from within you.

Think of someone you know – or even a celebrity you know about – who exemplifies the kind of contentment, surrender and peacefulness that comes when ego gives way to one's Higher Power. One such person who comes to mind is Eckhart Tolle, author of *The Power of Now*. His life-changing aha! moment caused him to realize that there is only now, and that the ego is unimportant. Imagine what it would be like to begin living that way now.

How would your business change if you didn't need personal validation through its achievements?

Ego demands its day in the sun, wants to protect the status quo – and usually encourages competition and separation so that it can attract more attention. Just as we explored cooperation taking the place of competition, a purpose-based business takes the place of an ego-driven business. The ego continually wants more, and is never satisfied. But purpose can be fulfilled in every moment, and result in an ongoing sense of contentment and contribution – even when on the way to a desired result.

To step fully into your authenticity as a Purposeful Entrepreneur™, you will need to be willing to polarize your customers, knowing some will *love* what you have to offer, and others may *hate* it. Dare to stop caring about what others think and stand up for what you are being called to deep within – you will find that those you attract *really* resonate with your products or services... and the rest were not really your customers to begin with.

Take your ego along for the ride, but let it sit in the back seat while your purpose and your Divine Contribution sit in the driver's seat. After all, the ego was never really in charge anyway, it was just a convenient container to be used for a period of development and set to the side.

46
Stretching and coasting

R ight now, you are either growing or dying. There is no in between.

Once we have been doing a particular kind of work for a while –
and that can include owning a business that has grown over a few
years – it is easy to fall into the trap of complacency. Things seem
to be going well, you are experiencing growth, and you know your
industry and your business inside and out. "So," you think to yourself,
"I'll just coast for a while."

The problem is, there is no "neutral gear" in life – so when you
decide to coast, you have inadvertently begun the process of dying.

Notice if there are any areas in your life or business in which you
have slipped into "coasting mentality" – and what results you are getting. Do you see corresponding drop in sales, decline in the quality
of those relationships, or decrease in the quality of your work or life
in those areas?

The "coasting mentality" is a sign that change is needed – and that
your purpose is calling you once again to express in a new or higher
way. Your job, once you notice this process beginning, is to say yes to
the change – even if you don't yet know what it is.

Ask yourself, "what is it that I am wanting more of – and that I no longer am feeling in that area of my life?" And then become open to its coming to you, in perhaps a surprising way – now that you have noticed that desire.

Without exception, successful people challenge themselves to new heights regularly. They seek out opportunities to stretch themselves, learn new things, try foods, activities or systems with which they are unfamiliar – and otherwise exercise the muscles of mental, physical and spiritual growth. In other words, they choose life on a moment by moment basis.

What have you always wanted to learn to do? What new business or hobby would be exciting and fun for you? Do it!

Set goals you don't think you can achieve – and then set an intention to do it! Price Pritchett points out in *You*[2] that if you already know how to achieve your goal, it will not lead to a quantum leap. You have to set it higher than what your stored knowledge and existing skills can achieve. That is the only way to achieve massive success and big jumps in performance and results.

Challenge yourself to an activity or experience that stretches yourself today – you'll be glad you did!

47
Staying in the question

Purposeful Entrepreneurs are known for being decisive and action-oriented. But at times, there is value in delaying resolution and "staying in the question" a bit longer.

This is especially true when the dilemma relates to a new business direction, yet another appearance of an ongoing issue you have encountered before, or a decision about what you can do to streamline a seemingly complex aspect of your company.

You will usually get pressure from staff, colleagues, partners and friends to decide quickly – it is ingrained in our culture. But if you do so *every* time, you leave no space for the big new insights that come from going beyond your normal comfort zone of thinking.

When I lead goal-setting workshops, I ask people to sustain the pace I have set and hold their attention on a given aspect of their strategy, intention or goal – even if they think they have exhausted all the possibilities in the first couple of minutes of brainstorming. By maintaining a calm, focused mind on an area such as new product development or key staff relationships, for three to five minutes or more, ideas will bubble up from your inner self that would not have otherwise appeared. And those ideas may be just what you need to explain what is not working – and what you need to be or do differently to improve it.

The type of question you "stay in" also matters! A closed-ended question that requires a simple yes or no answer will not lend itself to the insights you need. "Should I develop a new product for the abc market?" is such a closed-ended question. Instead, ask an open-ended question such as "What type of product would best serve the abc market?" or "What am I feeling led to create next?" or "How could I have both a AND b instead of having to choose between them?" These questions access the part of your mind that generates ideas, options and solutions. Its insights will amaze you!

Next time you have a decision to make, take a few minutes or an hour – or overnight – but longer than you normally would to make it. Ask your creative mind a question, and listen for the answers.

You might keep a notebook with you to jot down random insights that occur to you, both during the day and when you first wake up in the morning. Notice any people, books, magazines, movies, or other objects or experiences that particularly call to you. Keep your mind open with a calm neutrality, not a frantic "I must figure this out!" mentality. The calmer and more centered you can be, the more open you are to new ideas.

The questioning mind is a receptive mind. Let the insights in – they are waiting for you to allow them entrance.

48

Compassion

Your business is here to serve your customers. And if you do it in a compassionate way, it will multiply the value of your service and will irresistibly draw many other customers or clients to you. Why? Because compassion is all about emotions – your capacity (and that of your staff) to feel what your customer is feeling, and offer them a bridge from that emotional state to their desired emotional state. That bridge is your products and services.

The dictionary definition of compassion is "actively sympathetic concern for the suffering of another: mercy." And sympathy involves: "the capacity to share another's feelings."

So the marketing theorists were right: people buy based on their feelings. And if you don't connect with them on that level, they will say no and resist your offer, however tempting it may be.

Compassion allows you to meet your clients where they are, without judgment, and lovingly offer a solution to their most pressing issues or problems. When Jesus was speaking to the thief on the cross, the story goes that he did not condemn him for his acts, but said he would be with Jesus in paradise that day.

Whatever your company sells, ask yourself if you have broken it down to its most basic, fundamental benefits and parts, so that even someone with no knowledge of your industry could understand it. Most marketing and ad copy is written at the fifth grade level, since that is said to be the average comprehension level in the U.S.

Using a compassionate marketing approach, you connect heart to heart with your prospect, and make it easy and effortless for them to both understand and see the need for what you offer. The sale then simply becomes the next logical step in their thought process – a decision they want to make, instead of a "hard sell" that is unpleasant for both seller and buyer.

This is not to say you have to do business with everyone, or that you have to allow your staff (or yourself) to tolerate verbal abuse from customers or prospects. Instead, take a loving approach, tempered with good business practices and policies, and you will know which customers are – and are not – right for you.

Compassion should become a thread throughout all of your business dealings, not just during the sale itself. Manufacturing staff can think about the pleasure your product will bring, the transformation it will facilitate, or the joy that will result from someone purchasing and using it. Customer service staff can be pleasant, patient and focused on the individual customer – versus thinking of them as just a number or an anonymous call on the support line. Providers of your service – e.g., coaches, consultants, trainers etc. – can be aware both of the checklist of deliverables they are charged to deliver, and also of the emotional states and shifts that occur throughout a coaching session, a day-long seminar, or a consulting engagement.

Compassion can transform drudgery into magic, simply by shifting one's focus, one's attitude, and one's action toward love, service and a heart connection. And if everyone in your business does this, it will transform the business and some portion of the world too!

49
Social responsibility

One of the earmarks of a Purposeful Entrepreneur™ is a concern for the environment, and for mindful use of the Earth's resources. The time is long past when we can allow ourselves to be wasteful – or worse, compound the problem by creating pollution through our business activities – and get away with it. Even if we are not "caught" in the sense of being fined or charged with a crime, there is psychic harm to be done by not paying attention to whether we are nurturing and loving the earth through what we do for a living.

In addition to environmental sensitivity, being socially responsible means considering the interests of customers and others who are impacted by your business and its products. If your product carries danger or risk, provisions should be made for minimizing those risks and, should they manifest, for compensating damaged parties or otherwise taking care of that damage.

Traditional business theory tends to be a "we win, you lose" approach – and on many occasions it can be the customers or others outside the business that lose, or get the "short end of the stick" when they buy something that is not up to quality standards or pay more than they should.

When Johnson & Johnson had its Tylenol scare in 1982, when some bottles were tainted with cyanide, sales became nonexistent and the company lost a significant amount of money. But instead of running away, they became proactive, created a new type of tamper-resistant seals, and recalled their product. This restored their reputation as a trustworthy company – invaluable in view of the products they sell.

Other companies have made individual compensation in cases of damage – such as the US Airways flight that landed in the New York Harbor, all surviving but visibly shaken, in 2009. All passengers were given an individual payment to recompense them for the ordeal, which did not preclude legal action but was a gesture from the company of their willingness to make up for the inconvenience and trauma of the failed engines and the whole incident.

Social responsibility is an acknowledgement that everything is one, that it is all connected, and that you are willing to do your part to "do no harm" through the activities of your business.

How could you incorporate the notion of social responsibility into your business, both now and as it grows? Doing so builds good will and is actually a business advantage in the growing movement of spirituality and ecology.

50
Law of resonance

A ny time we have a new experience, our brain tries to connect it with a past similar experience. This is also true with our prospects: when they learn about our product or service, they mentally connect it to other similar (in their mind) products and services.

The Law of Resonance applies when a prospect or customer connects our offering – or something in it – to an *emotional* experience, not just a mental one. Because the statement, image or experience is tied to a previous emotional event, the prospect's reaction to your offer is exaggerated. You will hear either a huge "yes" or a huge "no", perhaps accompanied by tears or anger or another emotion, within them or within you.

So the Law of Resonance helps us understand unusually strong emotional reactions to what may be a simple business transaction. When this happens, ask yourself: "what prior experience is this bringing up or tied to?"

Now is the time to heal it – in fact, that is the purpose of the current experience. You or your salesperson may be in a position to shine the light on an old wound within the prospect and facilitate their healing, or it may be time for you to heal your own wound.

Resonance can be thought of as like the reverberation of sound from a gong or a powerful choir in a huge cathedral. As the sound reverberates, you physically feel the continued impact of the sounding of the instrument long after it occurs.

The purpose of resonance is transformation. And recognition and awareness are the first key to beginning the healing process. Notice that it is happening, release judgment that you "shouldn't" react this way – and be open to healing.

Second, clearly identify the past experience(s) that are triggering the resonance. What is the lesson here? What do all of these experiences have in common with the current one? Were your ideas discounted in all of the situations? Were you abandoned? Or taken advantage of?

Finally, forgive yourself and open to the perfect ritual or process or idea to help you move past this experience once and for all.

Being an entrepreneur means being open to growth... and it is in our growth that we heal, expand and transform. Resonance is just one tool to help us do so.

51
Being vs. doing

The Western culture is founded on a premise of doing – what you do determines your value and, for many, your self-worth.

Certainly, doing has its place. It is in many ways what has made America great. But like anything, taken to extremes it becomes a relentless driving force that can squeeze the very life out of our daily experiences.

Eastern philosophies embrace the idea of the yin, or feminine/receptive/being energy, is perfectly complimented by the yang, or masculine/active/doing energy. Many meditation practices are designed to create or allow space for the receptive energy to be activated – that calm, centered place where there is nothing to do, there is only to be. Cultivating this mindset helps the Purposeful Entrepreneur™ remain balanced in any business or life situation.

Any committed business owner needs to gain knowledge about business start-up, taxation, marketing techniques, sales strategies and other tactical aspects of running a business. These all help develop the yang side of the Purposeful Entrepreneur™ and set the structures in place through which a successful business can develop.

But without the yin/being aspect of owning a business also being developed, the sales and growth that do occur can be hollow.

Cultivate the ability to create space in your day, to receive praise, and to rest in the midst of your activity. As you give back to yourself, being the example of balance and nurturing that you advise others to also live, you will reap tremendous rewards both in results you obtain and in quality of life every day.

One of the most transformational questions you can ask yourself at any stage of your business – whether you are feeling overwhelmed by minutia or consumed with excitement over a new product launch – is this:

Who am I being in this moment?

And a related question: *Is who I am being now going to lead to the results I desire?*

If you are feeling overwhelmed and your being/presence is one of sarcasm, negative talk, sounding burdened, and emanating the message that "I don't like this," you will simply attract more overwhelm. It is a self-defeating cycle.

Instead, even in the face of overwhelm, you can choose to be calm, deliberate and centered. This mindset opens you to solutions, as you address one concern at a time, systematize and delegate – doing only what is truly in your areas of genius and strength. You are not driven by the situation; you are the calm "eye of the storm" in the midst of the situation. And others will follow your example.

52
Celebration

When was the last time you dedicated an hour, or even a day, to celebrating your success?

In our haste to "get more done," we can tend to jump right past the celebration of our accomplishment and be on to the next task or project.

Take time to celebrate both who you are and what you have done!

We know that being grateful for something draws more of that to us... and celebrating does the same thing. It is saying "thank you" to the Universe, to your staff, to yourself, and to all of the other people and forces that made launching your product, reaching your sales goal, filling your class, or whatever the achievement was a success.

In fact, when you set a goal, why not plan how you will celebrate its achievement in advance, as an additional incentive to your taking the steps needed to achieve it? Plan to take a long weekend in the mountains or at the beach, designate a spa day, or book a pleasure cruise. For a smaller achievement, perhaps you treat yourself to dinner at a favorite restaurant, a facial, or an afternoon browsing at your local bookstore. The larger the goal, the larger the reward.

Celebrating is more about the physical act itself (by now you have anticipated this as you have gone through this book, right?). It is about increasing your vibration to the energy of gratitude and joy – which will allow you to magnetize and manifest much more of what you want into your experience.

Think about a birthday party or other party you have attended. Don't you immediately feel better, and notice a smile coming to your face? That is the energy of celebration. And it is contagious!

Look for ways to build in celebration to every month's activities in your business, the achievement of every goal – and occasionally a "just because" celebration to acknowledge yourself, your staff and your business for who they are and all that they bring to your enterprise.

Celebrate your life and business – because you are worth it!

APPENDIX A:
What is a Purposeful Entrepreneur?

By Marcia Bench

A purposeful entrepreneur:

- Has identified his/her life purpose (or is ready to do so)

- Chooses to be an entrepreneur so that he/she can fully express that purpose through owning a business that does positive work to help others and make the planet a better place to live

- Incorporates the essence of his/her life purpose in every aspect of the business, from products and services sold to internal policies, communication both internally and externally, and even how income is handled (often giving a portion to charity from each sale)

- Believes in God or a Higher Power and spend time connecting with It daily; also believe that aligning with this Source and feeling supported by it - in every business activity - is critical to the business' achieving its spiritual mission and purpose

- Sees the conduct of the business as a spiritual activity, and connecting with customers as a sacred trust

- Realizes (or becomes aware) that challenges in the business are simply a reflection of the energy states and vibrational level of the business owner and its staff, and that to shift the flow of money or customer excitement or effectiveness of internal systems, the initial shift must be within the individuals working within the business

For coaching, classes, events and products designed to serve the Purposeful Entrepreneur, visit www.purposefulentrepreneur.com today or see the Resources section of this book.

ABOUT THE AUTHOR

Marcia Bench is a Marketing and Business Strategist for Purposeful Entrepreneurs, with more than 23 years' experience coaching, training, and speaking to entrepreneurs. A Master Purposeful Entrepreneur Coach,™ she has been coaching and consulting both individual and corporate clients since 1986. She is CEO of Purposeful Entrepreneur Enterprises, LLC http://www.purposefulentrepreneur.com, Founder/Director of Career Coach Institute, LLC, http://www.careercoachinstitute.com as well as other coaching companies.

A former attorney, Marcia has authored 22 other books. Her latest are *Career Coaching: An Insider's Guide* (High Flight Press 2008) and *Career Infopreneur's Success Roadmap* (High Flight Press 2007). She is currently working on the forthcoming *Purposeful Entrepreneur's Success Blueprint,* due out in summer 2009.

Marcia has been a featured speaker/trainer at over 500 local, regional and national conferences, as well as a guest on numerous television and radio programs. Her mission is to help individuals increase their sense of enjoyment and meaning in their work.

Marcia's coaching experience includes work with managers and executives from Fortune 500 firms in a variety of industries as well as dozens of business owners, professionals, and military officers entering the civilian workforce.

Prior to entering the coach training industry, Marcia was Senior Vice President in a dot-com career management firm for 4 years, and previously spent 10 years as President of New Work Directions, a business and consulting firm she founded. Ms. Bench developed her expertise in business start-up and management in part through her 4 years as a practicing attorney specializing in business and employment issues. She is a current member of the International Coach Federation.

Marcia's education includes a Juris Doctorate from Northwestern School of Law of Lewis & Clark College and a Bachelor of Science in Psychology from Western Oregon University. In addition, she is a Certified Career Management Practitioner through the International Board of Career Management Certification, a Certified Business Coach, a Certified Teleader and Master Certified Career Coach.

Purposeful Entrepreneur Enterprises, LLC

8269G SW Wilsonville Rd. #188

Wilsonville, OR 97070

Phone/Fax 877-51-PURPOSE

info@purposefulentrepreneur.com

www.purposefulentrepreneur.com

RESOURCES

I f you have enjoyed this book, we urge you to not stop here! Do
visit us online at http://www.purposefulentrepreneur.com for an
ever-expanding variety of resources to support you in your business
start-up, mindset shifts, and growing your company. You can even
learn how to coach Purposeful Entrepreneurs if you wish!

Following is a summary of the resources available as of this writing:

Coaching Services

Individual and group coaching services, both live and via telephone, are available with Marcia Bench (and, in the future, with
coaches trained through Purposeful Entrepreneur.com). We have
found coaching to be one of the most powerful and effective ways
to help you blend spirituality with sound business principles, using
regular mentoring and proven business models. For details on the
current programs, visit http://www.purposefulentrepreneur.com and
click on "coaching".

Live Events and Speaking Engagements

Marcia periodically offers teleclasses, as well as live workshops
and retreats for her clients, readers, and the public. (Private retreats

for your group can also be arranged upon request). To be notified of upcoming events, visit http://www.purposefulentrepreneur.com and click on "classes and events". Also register to receive our regular ezine, Purposeful Entrepreneur Times, there. And to hire Marcia to speak at your event or for a media interview, contact info@purpose-fulentrepreneur.com or call 877-51-PURPOSE.

Certified Purposeful Entrepreneur Coach Training and Certification

As the Purposeful Entrepreneur™ movement explodes, there is an rapidly increasing need for people to coach these unique thought leaders, coaches, speakers, authors and other independent business owners. We offer a 16-week certification program via teleclass (and in the future, via live training) by which you can become a Certified Purposeful Entrepreneur Coach™. A Master Purposeful Entrepreneur Coach™ training is also available for graduates of the initial level of training. For details, visit http://www.purposefulentrepreneur.com.

Purposeful Entrepreneur Books, CD's, and Other Products

Marcia's other books and many CD's, DVD's, pre-loaded mp3 player, and more are available both at http://www.purposefulentreprenuer.com/products.html and at her online store at http://www.coach-ingwebstore.com/. Volume discounts available for purchases by groups, for workshops, or to accompany Marcia's speaking engagements.

Business Building Support and Training

Marcia's CCC Business Acceleration System™, a two-volume manual for launching and marketing your coaching business, was newly revised in 2009. Teleclasses also available to guide you through these important stages of your business. Visit http://www.careercoachin-stitute.com/bas.html for details.

Purpose, Passion & Profits Mastermind

Would you like to stay on the leading edge of the emerging Pur-poseful Entrepreneur movement? Would you enjoy getting personal access to the leaders in this exciting community?

We have created our Purpose, Passion & Profits Mastermind program just for you — you get a monthly call with an expert hand picked by Marcia Bench, the founder of Purposeful Entrepreneur. com. We also send you the CD of the call — and occasional bonus gifts too! Get a two-month free trial membership at http://www. purposefulentrepreneur.com

Blog

Marcia also maintains a blog on Purposeful Entrepreneur trends at http://www.purposefulentrepreneurblog.com/ - feel free to register to be notified of new posts.

Career Coach Training and Certification

Marcia's blended learning approach to learning career coaching and getting certified have changed the lives of hundreds of people world-wide. If you want to learn coaching skills and develop career design and job search mechanics expertise — as well as practice coaching in real time and get feedback – you will want to explore our career coach training. You will join a worldwide community of coaches with a similar passion for career coaching and the same fundamental approach. Visit http://www.careercoachinstitute.com for details on training programs that lead to certification, as well as "a la carte" courses.

Don't see what you're looking for? Contact our customer service team at 877-51-PURPOSE (877-517-8776) within the U.S., or email us at info@purposefulentrepreneur.com. We are here to support your success!

Printed in the United States
213847BV00001B/17/P

9 780981 700533